AQA GCSE
ENGLISH AND ENGLISH LANGUAGE

UNIT 1 FOUNDATION TIER

Jo Heathcote
CONSULTANT: DAVID STONE

OXFORD
UNIVERSITY PRESS

Contents

Introduction

What is in your Unit 1 exam?

If you are following the AQA GCSE course in English or English Language, you will be sitting the Unit 1 exam. Unit 1 focuses on assessing your ability to read with understanding and to write for specific purposes and audiences. This Unit deals specifically with non-fiction texts – texts that are based on real life. The exam tests your ability to understand and produce non-fiction texts, which means that in different sections of the exam, you are both the reader and the writer. The exam is worth 40% of your total GCSE marks. It lasts 2 hours 15 minutes and is marked out of 80.

There are two sections in the exam:

- Section A: Reading. This is worth 40 marks. This is where you are the reader and your ability to understand a range of non-fiction texts is tested. You have to answer four questions (1a and b, 2, 3 and 4), based on three reading sources.

- Section B: Writing. This is worth 40 marks. This is where you are the writer and your ability to produce non-fiction texts is tested. You have to do two writing tasks: one shorter task worth 16 marks and one longer task worth 24 marks.

How to use this book

This book is divided into two sections – Reading and Writing – just like your exam.

In each section you will find chapters that focus on the different questions you will meet in the exam. Each chapter shows you how to approach the different questions in the exam and the key skills you need to demonstrate when writing your response. In each chapter you will find:

- a range of texts similar to those you will encounter in the exam

- an extract from the Mark Scheme that examiners use to mark your response, so that you can see exactly what skills are being assessed in each question

- sample questions

- advice on the key skills you need to be able to answer each question

- individual, pair and small-group activities to practise those key skills

- sample student responses

- advice on how to improve your responses

- opportunities for exam practice, self-assessment or peer-assessment.

Preparing for Section A: Reading

What is the content and focus of the exam?

Unit 1 Section A is worth 40 marks. It is where you are the reader and your ability to understand a range of non-fiction texts is assessed. You have to answer four questions (1a and b, 2, 3 and 4) based on three reading sources. These sources may be things like newspaper articles, information leaflets or webpages – the kinds of things we need to read and understand in our day-to-day life. They may also be texts you might choose to read in everyday life, such as magazine articles, travel writing, autobiographies or biographies. The sources may be linked by a theme.

How to use your time in the exam

You should aim to spend 1 hour 15 minutes on the Reading section (leaving 1 hour for the Writing section). The following provides a suggestion for how you could divide up your time in the Reading section of the exam:

Question and approach	Marks available	Suggested timing
Questions 1a and 1b: Read Source 1 then answer Question 1 (while the information is still fresh in your mind).	8 marks (4 marks for **1a** and 4 marks for **1b**)	15 minutes
Question 2: Read Source 2 then answer Question 2.	8 marks	15 minutes
Question 3: Read Source 3 then answer Question 3.	12 marks	25 minutes
Question 4: Answer Question 4 (there are no new source texts for this question).	12 marks	20 minutes

Each of the four questions is testing a different skill. It is essential that you attempt all four Reading questions in the exam in order to demonstrate all the necessary skills. If you miss out a question, you will not achieve the mark that you want.

Assessment Objectives (AOs)

Assessment Objectives are the skills being assessed during your GCSE course. Below is a list that shows you the AOs that you need to demonstrate in the Reading section of the Unit 1 exam:

AO number	AO wording	Question this AO applies to in Section A: Reading
AO2, i English AO3, i English Language	Read and understand texts, selecting material appropriate to purpose, collating from different sources and making comparisons and cross-references as appropriate.	You need to demonstrate this AO in Questions 1a and 1b, Question 2 and Question 4.
AO2, iii English AO3, iii English Language	Explain and evaluate how writers use linguistic, grammatical, structural and presentational features to achieve effects and engage and influence the reader.	You need to demonstrate this AO in Question 3 and Question 4.

By working through the Reading chapters of this book, you will practise these key skills and learn exactly where you need to demonstrate them in the exam in order to achieve your best possible mark.

Mark Scheme

The examiner uses a Mark Scheme to assess your responses. There are three main mark bands in the Mark Scheme for Foundation Tier: Band 1, Band 2 and Band 3.

Each mark band is summed up by a key word or words. For Reading, the key words are:

> Band 3: clear/relevant
>
> Band 2: some/attempts
>
> Band 1: limited

Each mark band consists of a range of skills, based on the Assessment Objectives above, which you have to demonstrate – if you imagine the skills inside the bands as rungs on a ladder, the further up the ladder you climb, the more demanding the skills become. This book aims to help you develop those skills to achieve the best mark of which you are capable.

Although the key words are common throughout the Reading section, the skills being tested in each question are different, so extracts from the Mark Scheme that examiners use for each question are included in each chapter.

What to expect in the exam

In the exam, you will have two non-fiction texts to read (Source 1 and Source 2) with three tasks to do (Questions 1a, 1b and 2), to show that you can:

- read a non-fiction text and understand it
- show your basic understanding by choosing some key pieces of information from it
- present that information in your own words
- use snippets of a text (quotations) to back up what you have understood
- show a more developed understanding by explaining a little of what the text means to you or suggests to you.

Practising the key skills

In the exam, Question 1a is based on Source 1 and is worth four marks. It is a simple task, designed to test that you can read the text and select four key pieces of information from it. The examiner will give you one mark for each correct piece of information you select.

However, simple tasks can sometimes cause problems and you might be wondering: How much should I write for Question 1a? Should I copy the right bits word for word? Should I use quotation marks?

You are being asked to do three things in your response to Question 1a:

- read the text carefully
- select four key pieces of information from it
- make a clear list of those four things.

A typical Question 1a might look like this:

> **1a** List four things you learn about ... from Source 1.

The topic of the question would be here.

Listing

Activity 1

Look at the sample exam question below:

> List four things you learn about rainbow toads from the article.

1. What is the focus of the question?

2. What are you being asked to select from the article?

Exam tips

Remember not to list just *any* four things from the source when answering Question 1a.

'Rainbow toad' rediscovered in mountains of Borneo

Scientists spotted a toad species from the 'top 10 most wanted lost frogs', last seen by explorers in 1924

The Sambas stream toad, or Bornean rainbow toad.

The first ever photographs of the rediscovered 'rainbow toad' last seen over four decades ago have been released by scientists exploring the mountains of Borneo.

In recent years, American-based organization Conservation International placed the Sambas stream toad, also known as the Bornean rainbow toad, on a world 'top 10 most wanted lost frogs' and feared it might be extinct.

Researchers found three of the slender-limbed toads living on trees during a night search last month in a remote mountainous region of Borneo, said Indraneil Das, a conservation professor who led the expedition.

Only illustrations of the toads previously existed, drawn from specimens collected by European explorers in the 1920s. Das said his team first decided to seek the toad last August, but months of searching proved fruitless until they went higher up the mountain range, which has rarely been explored in the past century.

'It is good to know that nature can surprise us when we are close to giving up hope, especially amid our planet's escalating extinction crisis,' said Robin Moore, a specialist on amphibians at Conservation International.

The toads found on three separate trees measured up to 5.1cm in length and comprised an adult male, an adult female and a juvenile.

Das declined to reveal the exact site of his team's discovery because of fears of illegal poaching due to strong demand for bright-hued amphibians. Researchers will continue work to find out more about the Borneo rainbow toad and other amphibians in the region.

Conservationists say many endangered animals in Borneo are threatened by hunting and habitat loss sparked by logging, plantations and other human development.

Now look at the response below, from Student A's answer to the Question 1a task on page 7.

Student Ⓐ

1. Rainbow toads are very rare. They haven't been seen for a long time.

2. We can now see photographs of rainbow toads, but before only drawings existed. ✗

3. Rainbow toads are 5.1 cm in length. ✓

4. Robin Moore said, 'It is good to know that nature can surprise us when we are close to giving up hope', when the toads were found. ✗

Exam tips

To improve on Student A's response, you need to work out the focus of the question as the first step to gaining full marks.

Activity 2

1. How many of Student A's answers above are definitely right?

2. If you were the examiner, how many marks would you award here?

3. Where in his answer has Student A made it difficult for himself to score full marks?

Ways of listing

When might you use a list? What purposes does a list have? Look at the three texts opposite and then complete Activity 3 below and Activity 4 on page 10.

Activity 3

1. Text A is a checklist of things to buy for a new pet puppy. It is a list of nouns – all the things the puppy will need. How is this list made more helpful for the reader?

2. Text B is a recipe. It contains two types of list.

   a) Can you explain what each list does in Text B?

   b) In the second list, what do you notice about the first word in each sentence? How does that help the list match its purpose?

3. Text C is a list of programmes in a TV guide.

   a) How is the information presented for the reader?

   b) How are the sentences in this list different from the ones in the recipe (Text B)? Is their purpose the same?

Text A

Shopping list for your puppy

- [ ] Puppy Food
- [ ] Puppy Treats
- [ ] Food and Water Bowls
- [ ] Toys
- [ ] Adjustable Puppy Collar
- [ ] Lead
- [ ] Pet ID Tag
- [ ] Puppy Bed
- [ ] Puppy Grooming Brush
- [ ] Teething Gel
- [ ] Chew Bone and Teether

Text B

Saucy Spring Greens

You can use any greens in this versatile dish (think spring greens, pointed cabbage, chard or green broccoli).

- 6 pork sausages (optional)
- 2 onions, finely chopped
- 3 garlic cloves, chopped
- 2 x 400g tins of whole tomatoes
- 2–3 mugs of greens, roughly chopped
- Sea salt and freshly ground pepper

Pop the sausages out of their skins. Pinch into bite-sized meatballs. Cook in a pan with the onions; season with pepper.

Stir in the garlic. Cook for a mo. Add the tomatoes; crush and break them up. Bubble away till the sauce is thick.

Fold the greens into the sauce. Cook till just soft and bright green. Add a pinch of salt and more pepper, if needed.

Text C

7.00   EMMERDALE

Charity presents Carl and Jimmy with the contract they need, in return for a 25 per cent stake in their business. Rachel accepts Jai's offer – provided she can choose the location, while Marlon feels positive after his meeting with the solicitor. (T,W,HD)

7.30   THE LAKES (8/12)

A local mountain-rescue team is called out to help a stranded family on the fells, and tour guide Sue Todd struggles to teach a Japanese colleague how to play crown green bowls. (R,T)

8.00   AGATHA CHRISTIE'S POIROT (3/4)

A guest at a village Halloween party boasts of having witnessed a murder years previously – and later meets a grisly end in keeping with the macabre spirit of the occasion. (R,T,W,HD)

10.00   ITV NEWS AT TEN, WEATHER

10.30   LOCAL NEWS, WEATHER

Activity 4

1. What different methods of listing are used in each text on page 9?

2. How does each method make the information clear?

3. Which method might be the most useful for presenting the information needed to answer Question 1a? Explain why.

Evaluating answers

Now look at Student B's attempt to answer the question: 'List four things you learn about rainbow toads from the article.'

Student **B**

1. Rainbow toads were last seen over forty years ago.

2. They are also known as the Sambas stream toad.

3. They were feared to be extinct.

4. Rainbow toads are at risk from poaching.

Exam tips

Be precise, sharp, and focus on the factual when selecting your points. Write four clear, accurate, simple statement sentences.

Student B has:

- used four clear, simple statement sentences
- not copied anything directly from the text
- kept the focus of the question in mind for every point.

Activity 5

Remind yourself of Student A's answer on page 8.

1. Who do you think has scored the most marks and shown they have understood both the question and the text: Student A or Student B?

2. Which student has been more efficient with their time? How can you tell?

Try it yourself

Now it's your turn! Read the article opposite and complete Activity 6.

Activity 6

List four things you learn about Portuguese men o' war from the article.

Surge in number of men o' war being washed up on beaches

Beachgoers and surfers are being warned of a surge in the number of deadly Portuguese men o'war off the coast of British beaches

The creatures, which resemble jellyfish, can inflict a severe and painful sting which in some cases can be fatal. Despite looking like a jellyfish, the Portuguese man o' war is not even a single creature but a floating colony of tiny marine organisms living together and behaving collectively.

They have been appearing in increasing numbers on beaches in south-west England, Wales and Ireland. According to the Marine Conservation Society, their increasing numbers on British beaches has been caused by global warming, and a rise in sea temperatures.

'Between 2003 and 2006 our survey received less than ten reports of Portuguese men o'war,' said Peter Richardson, from the MCS. 'Then between 2007 and 2008 sightings increased and in 2009 we received over 60 reports mainly from the west and south England and Wales – but also as far north as the Isle of Man.

'Last weekend a member of the public contacted Cornwall Council about a small number of what MCS identified as Portuguese men o'war washed up at Portheras Cove.

'We then had reports of similar sightings at Summerleaze and Widemouth beaches. Our most recent reports were yesterday.

'With the earlier standings in Ireland, these recent sightings could herald the arrival of more of the creatures as they get blown in from the Atlantic.'

Until recent years their normal habitats were the seas of the Florida Keys, the Atlantic Coast, the Gulf of Mexico as well as the Caribbean and the Pacific.

The man o'war earned its name because its airbag

The men o'war's blue tentacles can be over 30 feet long and deliver an agonizing and potentially lethal sting.

resembles the sail of a 16th-century Portuguese warship.

The airbag is about 12 inches long and 5 inches wide; beneath it are blue tentacles, which can be more than 30 feet long and deliver an agonizing and potentially lethal sting.

Rebecca Kirk, from Cornwall Council's public health and protection service, added: 'A sting may lead to an allergic reaction. There can also be serious effects, including fever and shock.

'Anyone who thinks they have been stung should seek medical attention immediately or contact NHS Direct.

'Even though they are washed up on the beach they can still present a possible risk of stinging and parents are advised to ensure children avoid touching them.'

Reading between the lines

Question 1b is also worth four marks, but it asks you to show different skills from Question 1a. This time, the focus is less precise. The question expects you to work out what is under the surface of the text. This is sometimes called 'reading between the lines'. For example, look at the question below:

1b What do you learn about the work of conservationists in '"Rainbow toad" rediscovered in mountains of Borneo' on page 7?

Re-read the article on page 7. You will notice that the article doesn't give you a lot of facts about the job of being a conservationist in Borneo, but by reading carefully we are able to discover a lot about the work they do. In this way, for Question 1b (and also for Question 2) you have to be a bit of a reading detective.

The notes below were gathered by Student A, who has been thinking about the question above.

They think about animals that might be extinct and try to find them.

They must take photos of animals because there is a picture.

They go on search expeditions to mad places like remote mountains.

'What do you learn about the work of conservationists from the article?'

They worry about things like poaching and hunting and logging.

Some of them are clever because it says one is a professor.

They have to work really hard to find the animals and even work at night.

Student A has worked out some ideas about what conservationists do, by finding clues in the article. However, if you look at the Mark Scheme the examiners use for assessing how well you have read with understanding, you can work out precisely *how* to present your detective work.

AO2, i English AO3, i English Language	Skills
Band 3 'clear' 'relevant' 4 marks	• clear evidence that the text is understood • engages with the text and makes inferences • offers relevant and appropriate quotations • makes clear statements on the work of conservationists
Band 2 'some' 'attempts' 2–3 marks	• some evidence that the text is understood • attempts to engage with the text and make an inference • offers a relevant quotation to support what has been understood • makes a statement on the work of conservationists
Band 1 'limited' 1 mark	• limited evidence that the text is understood • simple engagement with the text • offers some quotation, textual detail or copying out • simple reference to conservationists

Meet the examiner

Let's ask an examiner to explain how they use the Mark Scheme on page 13, so we can work out how to reach Band 3. Read the interview below aloud with a partner.

<table>
<tr><td>

Key term

Statement A clear sentence presenting one of your ideas in response to the task.

Quotation A small snippet of text presented in quotation marks (' ') used as evidence to back up your idea.

Inference An explanation of what you have been able to read between the lines or what has been suggested to you or implied by the text. This confirms your understanding.

</td></tr>
</table>

Examiner: We treat the marking grid like a ladder that students climb as they get better and better at showing their skills. Depending on the band you are aiming for – let's take Band 2 as an example – you start on the bottom rung and make a sensible **statement** in your own words to address the focus of the question. A clear, accurate point.

Student: A bit like in **1**a, you mean?

Examiner: Yes, that's right. But we want some evidence this time.

Student: What do you mean by 'evidence'?

Examiner: We want you to be able to support what you say, back it up with a snippet of the actual text – a **quotation**. That's step two of the ladder.

Student: Oh yes … we do that a lot when we write about poems and things … so you want it here too? How many should we use?

Examiner: Well, if you look carefully, Band 2 says 'quotation' but Band 3 says 'quotations', so that suggests we want more than one supported point for full marks. The quotation helps to show that you have read and understood the text itself.

Student: The third rung of the ladder makes no sense to me at all. What do you mean by 'engage', and what are '**inferences**'?

Examiner: It's not as tricky as it sounds. We just want to see what you have understood or taken away from the text. An inference is basically what your statement plus your quotation suggest to you as a reader. Kind of … what you've deduced from it, a possible explanation.

Student: Thanks for your help. We'd better let you get back to your marking.

Selecting relevant quotations

When you add a quotation to support your statements, you should choose the most appropriate snippet of text. The quotation should support your idea but not **paraphrase** it. Paraphrasing is when your statement and quotations sound almost exactly the same.

Student A has been working on this question:

> **2** What do you learn about the dangers the jellyfish present in 'Surge in number of men o' war being washed up on beaches' on page 11?

Student A has produced this practice statement plus quotation:

Student A

The jellyfish can give you a severe and painful sting, 'jellyfish can inflict a severe and painful sting.'

The statement almost copies out the quotation word for word – this is paraphrasing. It does not show enough understanding to reach beyond Band 1.

Activity 7

Look carefully at the statements below with a partner, and decide on a useful and appropriate quotation from the article about jellyfish to support each one.

> a) We learn the Portuguese men o' war are dangerous because they are described as '...
>
> b) We learn that the sting from these creatures is very serious and can even cause death, '...
>
> c) In the article, Rebecca Kirk explains the dangerous effects a sting can have, '...
>
> d) It seems that even the creatures that have been washed ashore can be a hazard for children playing, '...

Making inferences

Making inferences is a key skill for Questions 1b and 2.

Activity 8

Look at this advertisement, used as part of a Christmas appeal by a homeless charity. Read the text below, and then use the questions to help you work out what this advertisement is inferring and hoping its readers understand.

Why do you think the advert only refers to children? Does this make you think of homelessness in a different way? What is surprising about the number they use?

Why does the charity refer to Christmas morning as opposed to any other morning? What is the usual connection between children and Christmas?

What does the phrase 'hidden away' make you think of? Does it tell us anything about the problem of homelessness or the way it is dealt with?

How does the charity make you think more closely about children here? How important are these things in a child's life?

Why is this made to seem so serious and a bad thing? What are children normally taught about strangers?

What is implied here by using the two dates so close together?

75,000 of our children will wake up homeless on Christmas morning.

Yes, we're outraged too.

It's hard to believe, isn't it? But it's true. 75,000 homeless children are hidden away in hostels, B&Bs and other temporary accommodation across Britain.

Many will have spent years living in limbo – shunted from place to place and forced to leave friends, pets and toys behind. Some will be crammed into one room with their family – sharing beds with their siblings, and toilet and kitchen facilities with total strangers.

Such overcrowded, inadequate living arrangements take a terrible toll on a child's physical and mental health.

We saw conditions like this when we set up in 1966.

So we're outraged that it's still going on in 2012 – and we're asking everyone who shares that outrage to help us.

Activity 9

Write a clear paragraph explaining some of the inferences you have made from reading the advertisement. Choose the ideas you feel most confident about, use specific quotations from the advertisement to get you started and explain clearly what you have inferred by 'reading between the lines'.

So, to recap, a good method to use for both Question 1b and Question 2 is to:

- Make clear statements in your own words to address the focus of the question.

- Support what you have said by using a quotation which links to or backs up your point.

- Show your understanding by using inferences saying what the point and quotation suggest or imply, e.g. using:

Exam tips

Question 1b is only worth four marks, so you can't spend a lot of time on it. To hit all of the bullet points in the Mark Scheme on page 13, you should aim to make two clear, supported points, each with an inference.

This suggests that...

This implies...

This tells us that maybe...

Building an answer

Student A is going to try to use this good advice to shape his earlier ideas (see page 12) into a Band 3 response to the question:

1b What do you learn about the work of conservationists in '"Rainbow toad" rediscovered in mountains of Borneo' on page 7?

Activity 10

1. Work through Student A's notes on page 12 to find the points you feel he could present most clearly. Write a clear statement for each point.

2. Select a useful quotation from the text on page 7 that would support each point you make.

Activity 11

Now remind yourself of the sample 1b question and then look at Student A's write-up of one of his points below.

1. What skills can you can identify that Student A has covered so far, using the Mark Scheme on page 13?

2. Complete Student A's answer with a second point, a quotation and an inference to meet the Mark Scheme descriptors for Band 3. You can use Student A's notes on page 12 to help you.

1b What do you learn about the work of conservationists in '"Rainbow toad" rediscovered in mountains of Borneo' on page 7?

Student Ⓐ

Part of a conservationist's work involves going on expeditions, tracking down types of animals that may be in danger, for example they found rainbow toads, 'during a night search last month in a remote mountainous region of Borneo'. This suggests conservationists have to be brave and face tough conditions to do their job.

Try it yourself

Now it's your turn to practise all your Question 1 skills. Read the extract opposite and then try Activity 12.

Activity 12

Answer the following sample exam questions.

1a What do we learn from the article about the mystery boy? (4 marks)

1b What do you understand about the police investigation into the boy's identity? (4 marks)

German police release photo of mystery 'forest boy'

English-speaking teenager arrived in Berlin nine months ago saying he had been living wild and both his parents were dead

Berlin police have released a photograph of a mystery boy who claims to have spent five years living in a German forest, in the hope of establishing his identity.

The teenager, who has been nicknamed the 'forest boy', was discovered nine months ago when he turned up at Berlin's town hall carrying a rucksack and tent and saying he had walked for five days to get to Berlin. Calling himself Ray, he said both his parents were dead. The youth said his mother, Doreen, had been killed in a car accident, and that he had lived wild with his father, Ryan, in a German forest until his death last August.

Speaking English, Ray, who is believed to be 17, told authorities that he had buried his father before following his instructions to 'walk north until you reach civilization and then ask for help'. He does not know where his father died. He says he was born on 20 June 1994, but otherwise knows nothing about his identity. He wears an amulet bearing the initials D and R – believed to be those of his parents – around his neck. While he speaks English, experts who have heard his voice do not think it is his mother tongue.

Police are now hoping their international appeal for information will help to identify him, saying they have doubts about many aspects of his story.

'We have considerable doubts about his version of events,' the Berlin police spokesman told German media. 'Almost a year after he turned up the whole thing is still a complete mystery.' Investigators say they find it odd that the boy was so clean when he turned up in Berlin, and the two-man tent he had with him was in relatively good shape. He recalls details such as seeing his father get money 'out of a wall' and going shopping in the supermarket Lidl, but very little else.

Investigators immediately alerted Interpol to the boy's case last year. They carried out a DNA profile, which showed Ray most likely comes from Europe, and compared his fingerprints with databases worldwide, but to no avail. Releasing a photo – which was done only after in-depth discussions with the boy – is being seen as something of a last resort. Ray is described as being 1.8 metres (5ft 11in) tall with mousy brown hair and blue eyes. He has three scars on his forehead, three on his chin, and a scar on his right arm.

Ray is living in a care home for young people and can now speak German. But when questioned about further aspects of his life story, the boy simply replies that he cannot remember anything.

Reading Question 2

Audience The particular group of people a writer has in mind when they are writing a text.

Purpose The particular job a text is doing, for example, informing you, explaining something to you or persuading you.

Exam tips

The difference in marks here suggests that more detail is required than in Question 1b. The text will include many points that you can select. A useful method would be to choose four clear points for Question 2, support them with quotations and include your 'reading detective' inferences.

The Mark Scheme for Question 2 is almost identical to that for Question 1b. This suggests that you have to use exactly the same skills.

However, for Question 2 you have a text of a different genre to read – for example, instead of a news article, you might have a magazine feature, some travel writing or an extract from an autobiography. The Question 2 source material may have been written for a different **audience** and **purpose**. The examiner wants to see that you can read, understand and select material from a different kind of text, to show more of your reading abilities.

Another big difference here is the number of marks available: there are eight marks for Question 2 and only four marks for Question 1b.

More work on inference

Jackie Kay is a well-known poet and novelist. In the extract opposite, from her autobiography *Red Dust Road*, she describes a moped accident she had as a teenager. Read the extract and then complete Activity 13 on page 22.

From *Red Dust Road* by Jackie Kay

I was driving confidently towards Kirkintilloch when I decided I would take a turn-off to Lenzie that I'd never taken before. And that spontaneous decision changed my life. I was singing a Billy Ocean song, 'Love Really Hurts Without You,' though I wasn't thinking about anybody in particular. I looked behind me to check it was safe to change lanes, I'd looked in front and no one else was turning right. When I looked back up there was a car suddenly stopped in front of me, not indicating. I swerved to try and miss it. Then, according to eyewitnesses, I was thrown into the air. I hit another car coming towards me and then flew over the roof of a third car and rolled and rolled and rolled and landed outside a graveyard. (My mum said later, it was handy and they could have just thrown me over the wall.) I remember the sensation of rolling through the air, it seemed to take place in slow motion, and be almost dreamy. At some point I stopped and there were suddenly people around me. It occurred to me that I might actually be dead, since I couldn't speak or shout, but my thoughts were still going on. […]

A man is holding my leg in his hands. It feels like he is squeezing it. 'You're going to be all right,' he says. 'The ambulance is on its way.' [...] People on a double-decker bus are looking down at me from the top window as I am lying on the road looking up at them. They seem to be staring for ages. The bus is just stopped there in the middle of the road. There must be a traffic jam. (It takes me ages, looking back on this accident scene with me lying in the middle of the road, to realize that I am the jam. I am the traffic jam, and my blood is the jam on the road.) I wish they'd look the other way. I ask the man with the bald head and the anxious face to stop squeezing my leg. 'I'm not,' he says. 'I'm just trying to hold it. It's the pain.' Finally, it seems like ages, and it is apparently half an hour, an ambulance arrives. […]A man is in there already in a terrible state. His face is burnt with tar macadam. The ambulance men put my leg into a plastic balloon thing, […] and it is agony. They tell me it's a compound fracture and the bone has broken through the skin. […] The man with the burnt face makes jokes all the way to the hospital, though he must be in terrible pain. When we arrive at Glasgow Royal Infirmary, the ambulance men want to get him out first, but he says, 'No, after this young motorbike rider!' He tells me to take care and I tell him the same – injured soldiers that we are. He's made me brave.

An autobiography is a different kind of text from a news article. It includes the writer's thoughts and feelings as she describes her experiences. It is written in the first person (where the writer uses 'I' to describe their experience directly). As a result, we are likely to be able to infer more things from the text.

Activity 13

Having read the Jackie Kay extract, in pairs or small groups, copy and complete the table below. Think carefully about the quotations from the text. Note down everything that is suggested to you by the information Jackie Kay gives us in each quotation. An example has been completed for you.

Quotations from *Red Dust Road*	Reading between the lines: What is implied or suggested to you? What can you infer from this?
'I was driving confidently towards Kirkintilloch when I decided I would take a turn-off to Lenzie that I'd never taken before.'	This implies Jackie was on an unfamiliar or strange road. It seems like a snap decision and the fact she is doing it 'confidently' means she might be too confident or not prepared for any hazards.
'(My mum said later, it was handy and they could have just thrown me over the wall.)'	
'I remember the sensation of rolling through the air, it seemed to take place in slow motion, and be almost dreamy.'	
'The bus is just stopped there in the middle of the road. There must be a traffic jam. (It takes me ages ... to realize that I am the jam...)'	
'I ask the man with the bald head and the anxious face to stop squeezing my leg. "I'm not," he says. "I'm just trying to hold it..."'	
'He tells me to take care and I tell him the same – injured soldiers that we are. He's made me brave.'	

Step by step through the exam task

Read the following sample exam question and then complete Activities 14 to 16.

> **2** What do you understand about Jackie's moped accident from reading the text?

Activity 14

1. Choose four quotations from the table opposite. For each quotation, write an opening statement in your own words which shows what you understand about the moped accident. Remember to use **Standard English**.

2. Then link each of your opening statements to your chosen quotations. An example has been done for you, below.

Key term

Standard English
The version of English that uses the vocabulary, sentence structures and spellings that we all generally agree to be the correct ones.

This is the focus of the question.

The events Jackie describes are presented in your own words to show that you understand what she is telling you.

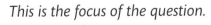

Jackie's moped accident happened when she decided to take a different route home: 'I was driving confidently towards Kirkintilloch when I decided I would take a turn-off to Lenzie that I'd never taken before.'

23

Activity 15

You have now collected four statements, each with a supporting quotation.

1. In pairs, look carefully at the suggested inferences you identified in Activity 13. Decide which inference fits best with each of your statements and quotations.

2. Add your chosen inferences clearly in Standard English to your answers. Make sure you link your quotations to your statements and use the method you learned for Question 1b (see pages 12–19). To help you, an example has been done for you, below.

The final sentence begins in a way that signals to the examiner that you are about to make an inference. It links carefully to the quotation by mentioning the word 'confident'.

Jackie's moped accident happened when she decided to take a different route home, 'I was driving confidently towards Kirkintilloch when I decided I would take a turn-off to Lenzie that I'd never taken before.' This suggests that even though Jackie was confident, taking an unfamiliar road presented her with unfamiliar hazards.

Activity 16

Swap your answers with a partner.

1. Identify the statements, quotations and inferences in your partner's work, using three different-coloured highlighters.

2. Look at the Mark Scheme below. Decide whether the work you are marking shows all the skills required to get top marks. If not, write down what you think it needs to do to earn top marks before swapping your answers back.

AO2, i English AO3, i English Language	Skills
Band 3 'clear' 'relevant' 7–8 marks	• clear evidence that the text is understood • clear engagement with the text and makes inferences • offers relevant and appropriate quotations • makes clear statements on Jackie's moped accident
Band 2 'some' 'attempts' 4–6 marks	• some evidence that the text is understood • attempts to engage with the text and makes an inference • offers some relevant quotations to support what has been understood • makes some statements on Jackie's moped accident

Try it yourself

Now it's your turn to attempt a Question 2-style exam task. Remind yourself of the Mark Scheme on page 25. Read the extract opposite and then complete the task below.

Exam tips

- Remember to make clear statements backed up by quotations from the text.

- Put all your quotations in quotation marks to show they are from the text.

- Remember to accompany each statement plus quotation with something you have inferred from the text – something it has suggested to you.

- Aim to write your four collections of statement plus quotation plus inference in crisp, clear Standard English.

Activity 17

Read the extract from *Pelé: The Autobiography*, in which the world-famous Brazilian footballer talks about his childhood, and answer the question below.

> **2** What do you understand about Pelé's childhood from reading the extract? (8 marks)

From *Pelé: The Autobiography* by Pelé

I suppose having a footballer as a father was the start of it. Most sons want to be like their fathers and I was no exception. Dondinho scored lots of goals and everyone said he was good. I never thought of playing for Brazil, or of winning the World Cup or anything like that. I just told my friends, 'One day, I'm going to be as good as my dad.' And Dondinho was a good man, too: a marvellous father. And despite the fact that his football never brought in much money, because it was the game that he played, I guess I became fascinated by it too. It was in the genes.

And this was Brazil, remember. Football was everywhere when I was growing up. As I played with friends in the yard or the street, there were always games going on around us, usually organized by slightly bigger boys. My friends and I were desperate to take part, but it wasn't easy to get a place in the teams; they said I was too skinny. It's true, I was small and scrawny as a boy. Those were the first times I was barred from a game, and if anything it only made me want it more. The boys we so wanted to join were maybe ten, a few years older than us, and they thought they were kings of the road. This didn't stop us – the young ones – from planning our own revolution. We would hang around outside the pitch and when the ball came out we wouldn't return it, but would start playing with it ourselves. It earned us many slaps and kicks up the backside. […]

[…] We had no kit, of course – not even a ball, and we had to make do with stuffing paper or rags into a sock or stocking, shaping it as best we could into a sphere and then tying it with string. Every now and then we would come across a new sock or bit of clothing – sometimes, it must be said, from an unattended clothes-line – and the ball would get a little bit bigger, and we'd tie it again. Eventually, it came to resemble something close to a proper football.

Which is more than could be said for the pitch – my first matches were held in the […] street […]: 'goalposts' of old shoes at either end, […] the touchlines more or less where the houses began on either side. But for me at the time it was like the Maracanã, and the place where I began to develop my skills. As well as the chance to spend time with friends and test myself against them, this was when I first learned the joy of controlling the ball, making it go the way I wanted it to, at the speed I wanted it to – not always easy with a ball made of socks. Playing football soon became more than just a pastime, it became an obsession.

What to expect in the exam

In the exam you will be given a third piece of source material to read: Source 3. You will be given one task to do – Question 3 – to show that you can:

- read a non-fiction text and select some of its important or interesting language features

- show your knowledge about language by presenting the examiner with examples of those features from the text

- explain why you think the writer chose each of the features and how a reader might feel when they read them.

Practising the key skills

Question 3 is worth 12 marks. In order to do well in Question 3 you need to have some knowledge about language.

A typical Question 3 will look like this:

---

3 Now read **Source 3**. How does the writer use language features in the text?

Remember to:
- give some examples of language features
- explain the effects.

Activity 1

Jot down what you understand about these two key terms:

a) language features

b) effects.

Look at the Mark Scheme below:

AO2, i, iii English AO3, i, iii English Language	Skills
Band 3 'clear' 'relevant' 9–12 marks	• clear evidence that the text is understood in relation to language features • developed comment on the effects of features of language • supports response with relevant quotations • clear examples of language features
Band 2 'some' 'attempts' 5–8 marks	• some evidence that the text is understood in relation to language features • some comment on the effect of features of language • attempts to support response with usually relevant quotations • some examples of language features
Band 1 'limited' 1–4 marks	• limited evidence that the text is understood in relation to language features • simple generalized comment on the effect of features of language • simple support with textual detail • simple mention of language/language feature

Just as for Questions 1b and 2, the Mark Scheme is like a ladder you have to climb. You could think of the method for this question like this:

Step 1: Find a language feature that is used in the text.

Step 2: Give an example of it.

Step 3: Write about the effect of the language feature in the text and on the reader.

If you are trying to show 'clear examples of language features' for Band 3, you should aim to identify about six key features with examples and effects for the 12 marks.

To be able to answer Question 3 correctly, you need to know:

• what language features are
• what it means to comment on their effect.

What are language features?

To begin with, you need to understand that language is made up of words and phrases.

Our language is made up of words and phrases that we use all the time without really thinking about them. However, when we are analysing language we need to take a more technical approach.

Words do different kinds of jobs. Although we don't often think about this when we are using words to speak, we need to think about it when we are using words to write. This is particularly true when we are analysing the choices of words in something someone else has written.

Understanding language features

All the words we use can be organized into eight categories. At GCSE level, it's useful to know about five of these: nouns, pronouns, adjectives, verbs and adverbs – you've probably heard these terms, but can you remember the importance of each?

Activity 2

Look at the table opposite. It includes examples of each of the eight different categories of words.

Working in a small group, explain what kind of job each category might do in a sentence. You may find it helpful to use examples.

Three have already been done for you, leaving the five you are going to be working with in this chapter for you to discuss.

What job does each of these key word categories do?

Word category	Examples	Explanation
determiners	the, a, some	A word that goes before a noun to show either a specific thing: 'Can I have *the* book?' or anything in a group: 'Can I have *a* book?'
nouns	house, table, book, road	
verbs	run, cries, is, jumping, shines	
adjectives	happy, yellow, shiny, rough	
adverbs	joyfully, sadly, angrily	
prepositions	on, above, below, around	Prepositions give us information about where things are: 'The house is *around* the corner.' 'Your coat is *on* the peg.'
pronouns	his, hers, its, I, you	
conjunctions	and, but, so	These words join parts of sentences together: 'The garden was wet *and* muddy.' 'The night was dark *but* a shaft of white moonlight shone on the path.'

Activity 3

Look at the sentence below. It contains all eight of the word categories in the table above.

Identify examples of your five key word categories:

1. Nouns   **4.** Adverbs

2. Verbs   **5.** Pronouns

3. Adjectives

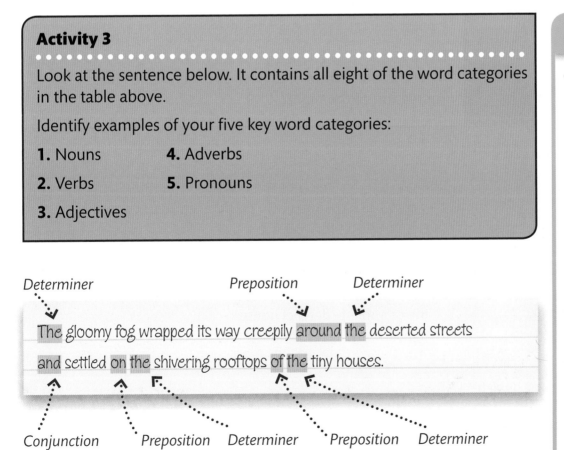

Determiner   Preposition   Determiner

The gloomy fog wrapped its way creepily around the deserted streets and settled on the shivering rooftops of the tiny houses.

Conjunction   Preposition   Determiner   Preposition   Determiner

Exam tips

You may have noticed that there are a lot of determiners and prepositions here, but they are not the most interesting parts of the sentence. The most interesting parts are the ones you have been working on.

In the exam, it is your job to select the most interesting uses of language – that is, the most important choices of words or phrases – to analyse in your answer.

More on language skills

Noun phrases

Linking a noun (a naming word) and an adjective (a describing word) together creates a noun phrase:

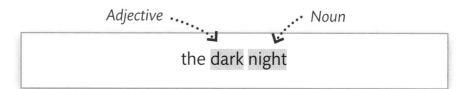

Adjective .... *Noun*

the dark night

The magic happens when you change the adjective – you can change the 'mood' or the atmosphere in the text.

Look at the examples below and discuss what impression is given by each one.

> the black, stormy night

> the black, starry night

Think about how changing the adjective changes the picture we see in our mind's eye. How does each one change our impression of the night?

Activity 4

1. Work with a partner. For each of the nouns in the table below, write three noun phrases, each using a different adjective. The first example has been done for you.

Noun	Noun phrase
house	the white, seafront house the crumbling, derelict house the dark, ivy-covered house
forest	
beach	
garden	

2. In small groups, discuss the different pictures you have created by changing the adjectives in your noun phrases.

Proper nouns and pronouns

Sometimes the nouns in a text have a special job to do:

- Proper nouns always have capital letters. They tell us the names of people, places, days of the week, months of the year and titles of books, plays and films.

- Pronouns are the words we use instead of proper nouns. We might replace our name with 'I', or someone else's name with 'he', 'she', 'you'. We might replace a place name with 'its'. When a text uses the word 'you' or 'your' to seem like it's speaking to you, this is called direct address.

Activity 5

1. Read the piece of travel writing on page 34 about Copenhagen and decide whether the highlighted words are:

- noun phrases
- proper nouns
- pronouns.

Collect your findings in a table like this. An example of each has been done to get you started.

Noun phrases	Proper nouns	Pronouns
a garish wonderland	Copenhagen	our

2. Choose two of the noun phrases you have collected and explain what you see in your mind's eye when you think about it.

3. Why does the writer use the long list of proper nouns in the second sentence?

4. By using proper nouns like 'December' and 'Christmas', what impression is the writer creating of Copenhagen?

5. Try to identify some of the interesting **verbs** the writer has used to create a sense of the action and movement.

6. Discuss with a partner or with your class what image is created by verbs like:

- '*dusted* with frost'
- 'snow *swirled*'
- '*squeezed* into scruffy bars'
- '*stumbling* home'.

Key term

Verb An action or doing word, e.g. laughing, hop, sleep.

I love Copenhagen. Edinburgh, Bologna, New York, Amsterdam … all cities I like, but Copenhagen I have a proper, heart-pounding crush on. It was love at first sight. My first time, it was December and bitterly cold. The cobbled streets were dusted with frost and snow swirled over the million fairy lights in the Tivoli Gardens, a garish wonderland of roller coasters and Christmas stalls. We took freezing walks along buzzing shopping streets, and bought tasteful Christmas decorations. We stopped for reviving glasses of mulled wine in tiny basement bars lit only by firelight and candles, where we sat at long wooden tables and made friends with our neighbours.

At night we partied with the young and the beautiful, squeezed into scruffy bars and slick, minimalist nightclubs before stumbling home via a hot dog stand for a huge midnight snack. It was bliss. I was smitten. And as with all great love affairs, I longed for more.

Key term

Purpose The particular job a text is doing, for example, informing you, explaining something to you or persuading you.

Exam tips

Avoid vague comments like 'It keeps the reader reading on' and 'It gets the reader hooked'. Sentences like this are meaningless, as they do not refer precisely enough to the language feature you are writing about. They show you are only thinking at a 'limited' Band 1 level.

When writers use particular features, they do this to make the text fit its **purpose**. For example, in the text above:

The writer is both *informing* us about Copenhagen – for example, that it has 'shopping streets' and 'bars' – and making the place sound appealing.

By making it sound appealing, we may want to visit ourselves and so the language features are *persuading* us.

The *noun phrases* add to the appeal because they *describe* different aspects of Copenhagen in a way that makes them sound attractive or exciting.

The use of interesting *verbs* helps us to imagine the kinds of things we could do in the place or the actions we might see.

By explaining clearly what you, as the reader, might see in your mind's eye when you have identified language features, you are beginning to comment on the effect of the language.

Look at the sample exam question below. It is based on an extract from a gardening book for children on page 36. The extract provides information and then gives instructions on how to complete a project.

---

3 How does the writer use language features in the text 'Flower friends' on page 36?

Remember to:
- give some examples of language features
- explain the effects.

Activity 6

Read the text on page 36 carefully. Then work with a partner to make notes on the following to help you to plan an exam-style answer.

1. Look at the list of things you need in order to undertake the project. Which language feature best describes the words in this list?

2. Look at the list of plants you might use. Which language feature best describes the words in this list?

3. Read the instructions at the bottom of the page. What do you notice about the verbs? Where do they come in the sentence? How would you best describe these sentences? Are they:

- making a clear **statement**?

- asking you to do something or giving you a **command**?

- asking you a question?

4. Which pronoun is used in the text? Try to explain why it is used.

5. Find one or more examples of adjectives in the text. This text gives instructions on how to make something. Why might the writer still have wanted to use describing features like adjectives?

Key term

Statement A sentence that declares something and presents it as fact or opinion.

Command A sentence which gives us an order or makes us do something. It has a verb as its first word to emphasize the thing it wants us to do.

★ easy as ABC | when to plant: **late spring–summer** | time to grow: **none**

Flower friends

Some common plant names include a person's name and and it's fun to collect a quirky group of 'friends' together. You could even make name tags to put in their pots, if you like.

you will need
- trowel
- gravel
- colourful glazed pots, 3
- peat-free potting compost with added loam (soil mix)
- plants with people's names (see Plant List)
- split cane (stake),, protector
- watering can

compost

gravel

plant list
* **Black-eyed Susan**
  Thunbergia alata
  Suzie hybrids
* **Busy Lizzie**
  Impatiens New Guinea hybrids
* **Creeping Jenny**
  Lysimachia nummularia
* **Flaming Katy**
  Kalanchoe blossfeldiana
* **Jacob's ladder**
  Polemonium
* **Sweet William**
  Dianthus barbatus

1 Using a trowel, put a layer of gravel in the bottom of each of the pots, for drainage.

2 Add enough compost to allow the surface of the root-balls to sit about 2cm (¾in) below the rim of the planter. This makes watering easier.

3 Position the flaming Katy plants. Squeeze a couple of extra plants in for a bold display.

4 Plant the tall, annual climber black-eyed Susan in a separate pot. You can grow this from seed in spring or buy plants to train up canes.

5 Top up the compost in all the pots, working it down the edges.

6 Insert the cane in the pot containing the black-eyed Susan. Check that a suitable cane protector is in place. Water thoroughly and stand in a warm, sheltered spot.

TOP TIP
▶ These plants can also be grown on a well-lit windowsill or in a conservatory (sunroom). Pinch off fading blooms and use a liquid feed for flowering plants every two weeks. Water flaming Katy sparingly.

28   flower power

(!) = Watch out! Sharp or dangerous tool in use.   (🖐) = Watch out! Adult help is needed.

Now look at how Student A has attempted the question below about 'Flower friends'. Then complete Activity 7.

3 How does the writer use language features in the text 'Flower friends' on page 36?

Remember to:

- give some examples of language features
- explain the effects.

Student A

This text tells us about planting flowers. It uses language to inform us about flowers and what to do with them. It makes the reader want to join in and do the project for themselves. The language tells us all about flowers and it makes it really easy for little kids to do the project. They use numbers so the instructions are step by step. This makes it seem simple and the language is simple too, so it's a really no nonsense text that gets straight to the point.

Activity 7

If you look back at the Mark Scheme on page 29, which mark band do you think Student A would be in?

To help you, the examiner says:

> *This student has tried to talk about language in this answer. However, he is unable to identify any language features and only mentions language in a general way. He gives no examples of the types of language he is talking about. He tries hard to say something about the effect, for example recognizing how the simple vocabulary might make it easy for a young child to do the project, but again this is working in a very simple, generalized way.*

Now look at the answer that Student B has started:

Student B

The text uses language to give us information. It uses nouns like 'trowel', 'gravel' and 'watering can' to inform the reader about the things they will need if they want to do the project. It doesn't just tell the reader to buy any old plant; the writer uses proper nouns 'Busy Lizzie' and 'Flaming Katy' to tell us precisely which flowers would be best for the project.

When it gives the instructions, the text uses verbs like 'Squeeze,' 'Top up' and 'Check' to begin the sentences. This turns the sentence into a command so that the reader will know exactly what it is they have to do to make the flowerpots.

It also uses adjectives like 'fun' and 'quirky'. I think this is to make this more appealing to children as this is a gardening book for children.

Student B has:

- identified four language features and named them correctly
- given more than one example of the features she has identified
- tried hard to give a reason for every language feature being there.

Student B is working at a Band 3 level here.

> **Peer-assessment**
>
> **Activity 8**
> ●
>
> 1. Using Student B's method, write your own answer to the question on 'Flower friends' on page 37 using the notes you collected in Activity 6.
>
> 2. Swap your answer with a partner and try to identify which band of the Mark Scheme your partner's work is in and why.

Language which creates special effects

Alliteration, simile, metaphor, personification and onomatopoeia

When we study poetry, novels or short stories, we learn to look out for the special effects that language can create. Non-fiction writers use these too, to help them describe or explain things, or to persuade their readers.

Alliteration: This is a sound pattern you can create by using words in a sentence which all begin with the same letter; for example, 'the silent stars twinkled over the solemn river'.

Simile: This is a way you can compare two things using the words 'like' or 'as'; for example, 'His room looked like a dumpsite.'

Metaphor: This is an interesting way of making a comparison. This time you say that an object actually is something else; for example, 'Her home was a prison.'

Personification: This gives human qualities to animals or objects – using this, you can bring an object to life like magic! For example, 'The table groaned under the weight of the cake.'

Onomatopoeia: This is another sound effect where the word you use actually sounds like the noise you want to describe. For example, 'smash', 'bang' or 'crackle'.

Activity 9

Look at the examples below. Identify what types of language features they use (using the explanations on page 39 to help you).

1. The moon's a balloon.

2. The twig snapped underfoot.

3. The furtive fox padded silently through the forest glade.

4. The perfect fried egg shone back at me like a sunny morning.

5. The wind raced around the house and the trees outside groaned and begged to come in.

Activity 10

1. Read the extract from *Boy*, opposite. In this passage, Roald Dahl describes his childhood visits to his grandparents in Norway.

2. Make a copy of the table below. For each language feature, find an example from the text.

Language feature	Example	Effect(s)
Simile		
Alliteration		
Metaphor		
Onomatopoeia		

Check you are correct by referring back to the definitions on page 39.

3. In the third column of your table, explain the effect of each language feature you have found by writing down what it makes you think of, feel or imagine.

4. Next, identify three more interesting language features from this extract. Add their names to the first column of your table. For each one:

- give the example you have found

- explain its effect – what does it make the reader think of, feel or imagine?

From _Boy_ by Roald Dahl

This was a Norwegian household, and for the Norwegians the best food in the world is fish. And when they say fish, they don't mean the sort of thing you and I get from the fishmonger. They mean _fresh fish_, fish that has been caught no more than twenty-four hours before and has never been frozen or chilled on a block of ice. I agree with them that the proper way to prepare fish like this is to poach it, and that is what they do with the finest specimens. And Norwegians, by the way, always eat the skin of the boiled fish, which they say has the best taste of all.

So naturally this great celebration feast started with fish. A massive fish, a flounder as big as a tea-tray and as thick as your arm was brought to the table. It had nearly black skin on top which was covered with brilliant orange spots, and it had, of course, been perfectly poached. Large white hunks of this fish were carved out and put on to our plates, and with it we had hollandaise sauce and boiled new potatoes. Nothing else. And by gosh, it was delicious.

As soon as the remains of the fish had been cleared away, a tremendous craggy mountain of home-made ice-cream would be carried in. Apart from being the creamiest ice-cream in the world, the flavour was unforgettable. There were thousands of little chips of crisp burnt toffee mixed into it (the Norwegians call it _krokan_), as a result it didn't simply melt in your mouth like ordinary ice-cream. You chewed it and it went _crunch_ and the taste was something you dreamed about for days afterwards.

Key term

Repetition When a word or phrase is included more than once in a text.

Repetition

Student B has been practising her Question 3 exam skills using the Roald Dahl text on page 41. One of the additional language features that this student has identified is **repetition**. Here is what she has written so far:

Language feature + example

Student B

Roald Dahl begins this extract with a focus on the noun 'fish'. He uses

Language feature + examples

repetition of the words 'fish', 'fishmonger' and 'fresh fish'. I think he does this to try and show us how important fish is to Norwegians and what an important

Sensible and valid comment on effect

part of their culture it might be. Another reason why I think this is that he goes on to describe a celebration meal involving fish.

The writer describes the fish they eat at the meal using similes: 'big

Language feature + examples

as a tea tray' and 'as thick as your arm'. This is to give the reader a visual comparison so that we can judge just how big this 'massive fish' was.

Begins to comment on effect

Activity 11

Complete Student B's practice answer using the ideas you gathered in Activity 10. Use Student B's formula:

Language feature + Example + Comment on effect

Key term

Direct address When a text uses the word 'you' or 'your' to make it seem like it is speaking to you.

Listing A sequence or pattern created by placing words with something in common together separated by commas. Things are often listed in groups of three for effect.

Direct address and listing

When texts are trying to persuade us, they use many of the language features we have learned about already, but they often use them in particular ways.

Look at the text opposite advertising a Christmas pantomime. It uses the pronoun 'you' in every paragraph. This technique is called **direct address**.

The text also uses **listing** as a technique.

Activity 12

1. How does the use of direct address make you feel as a reader? Why do you think the text is trying to 'speak' to you directly?

2. Find three places in the text below where either **nouns** or **proper nouns** are listed. What do you think the impact of this might be?

Key term

Noun A word which names an object, emotion or thing.

Proper noun A word or words which name something specific, such as people, places, days, months, titles of books, plays and films. All proper nouns begin with a capital letter. Your name is a proper noun.

The adventures of Peter Pan, Wendy, Captain Hook and, of course, Tinkerbell will be brought to you as never seen before in a marvellous new version of J.M. Barrie's timeless story.

In this enchanting tale of the boy who refuses to grow up, Peter Pan and the Lost Boys introduce Wendy Darling and her brothers to a magical world of adventure in Neverland – where children stay young forever and are free from adult rules. This fantastical land is home to mermaids, fairies and crocodiles as well as swashbuckling pirates whose bloodthirsty swordplay will have you on the edge of your seat!

Peter Pan will be brought to you by the same creative team behind last year's box office smash *The Wonderful Wizard of Oz*. With original music performed live by a cast of talented actor-musicians, a cast of local young performers and just a sprinkling of fairy dust, this year the Octagon will take you on the festive adventure of a lifetime!

Being clear about effect

The word 'effect' can mean different things. Look at the sentences below.

Here the word 'effects' seems to mean consequences or results.

Now the word 'effect' seems to mean the mental or emotional impression something might have on us.

1. The effects of global warming could be devastating for the planet.
2. Winning the gold medal had an amazing effect on the sprinter.
3. This wasn't the effect I was hoping to create.

Lastly, the word 'effect' seems to relate to someone's intentions or a message they are trying to get across.

When we talk about the effects of language, we are thinking about language in all of these ways.

Do the language features in a text have 'consequences'? For example, do they make us *behave* in a certain way? Instructions, for example, make us 'do' actions.

Do the language features leave a 'mental or emotional impression' on us? For example, descriptions might make us *feel* a certain way or *imagine* something more clearly.

Do the language features relate to a 'message'? Do they make us *respond* or *think* in a particular way? Persuasive texts often make us want to buy something or support a charity appeal.

Activity 13

Some of the language features and examples from the *Peter Pan* pantomime flyer on page 43 have been collected for you in the table below. Discuss why each language feature has been chosen. Consider how each language feature might make you:

- respond
- feel
- behave
- imagine
- think.

Language feature	Example	Possible effects
Proper nouns	Peter Pan, Wendy, Tinkerbell	
Direct address	... brought to you ... on the edge of your seat	
Noun phrases	fantastical land bloodthirsty swordplay magical world	
Listing	mermaids, fairies and crocodiles	
Alliteration	... swashbuckling ... swordplay ... seat	

How does the language feature make me **think**?

How does the language feature make me **feel**?

What does the language feature make me **imagine**?

How does the language feature make me **behave**?

How does the language feature make me **respond**?

Step by step through the exam task

Look at the sample exam question below; then read the Brownsea Island text and complete Activity 14 (on page 48).

3 Read this information leaflet for visitors to Brownsea Island in Dorset. How does the writer use language features in the text?

Remember to:
- give some examples of language features
- explain the effects.

Explore Brownsea Island

National Trust

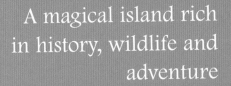

A magical island rich in history, wildlife and adventure

Enjoy the stunning coastal views and walks.

Discover secluded spots perfect for picnics.

Go wild about wildlife with family trails, tracker packs and events.

"The best place for seeing wildlife in Dorset"

That's how Bill Oddie described Brownsea Island. Whether you love nature or just want to escape from the stresses of modern life, Brownsea Island is the perfect place to explore, relax and take time out – here are some of the things you'll enjoy on Brownsea Island this year.

Walking with wildlife

Explore wonderful woodland, heathland and coastal walks with friends and family and discover Brownsea's unique wildlife along the way. Spot avocets, terns and godwits* on the lagoon and look out for the elusive and rare red squirrel. We have a range of self-led walks, daily introductory walks and an exciting range of guided walks throughout the year.

* all names of birds

History and mystery

Go to the visitor centre to discover more about some of the people who have lived on the island and made Brownsea their home. From a hermit in the middle ages to the reclusive Mrs Bonham Christie there is plenty of history and intrigue.

An island of adventure

Pre-booked youth and school groups can stay on our campsite and youth hostel accommodation. Groups can try their hand at archery or low ropes or discover more about the island with orienteering activities. We also offer a range of activities for families to get involved in so why not find out more about our den building and outdoor activity days – helping you to get closer to nature and spend some time in the great outdoors!

Taste of the place

Enjoy delicious food and drink in the Villano Café and admire stunning harbour views.

Take home a memory

Shop for great gifts and treat yourself to some local Dorset goodies and red squirrel souvenirs.

Activity 14

1. A number of interesting examples from the text have been collected in the mind-map below, based on the text on pages 46–47. Draw your own mind-map and label the examples with the name of a language feature. You could work on this with a partner.

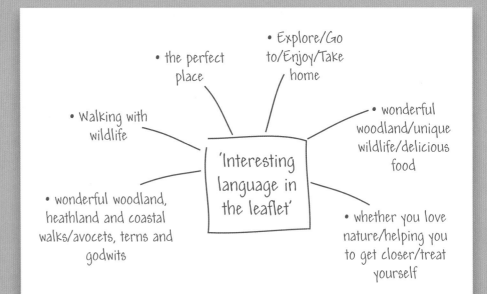

- the perfect place
- Explore/Go to/Enjoy/Take home
- wonderful woodland/unique wildlife/delicious food
- Walking with wildlife
- 'Interesting language in the leaflet'
- wonderful woodland, heathland and coastal walks/avocets, terns and godwits
- whether you love nature/helping you to get closer/treat yourself

2. For each of the six language features, write a clear sentence identifying the feature and adding the example. One has been done for you below.

> The writer uses verbs to open sentences and begin headings, such as 'Explore', 'Go to', 'Enjoy' and 'Take home'.

3. Add a clear and precise comment on the possible effect each language feature might have on the reader.

Remember to consider how the feature might make you *respond*, *behave*, *think*, *feel* and *imagine*, and link these ideas to the purpose of the text if you can. An example has been completed for you opposite.

Clear, accurate examples ⋅ *Language feature identified*

The writer uses verbs to open sentences and begin headings, such as 'Explore', 'Go to', 'Enjoy' and 'Take home'. These create commands for the reader and, in effect, give the reader things to do. This can be very persuasive as it emphasizes that there are plenty of activities to do on Brownsea Island.

Comment on effect

Link to purpose

Developed comment on effect

Activity 15

Peer-assessment

Exchange your response to the task with a partner. Using the Mark Scheme on page 29, try to identify the following in your partner's work:

	Yes ✓	No ✗
Has your partner identified any language features (rather than just mentioning language generally)? This will help you decide between Band 1 and Band 2.		
Has your partner managed to clearly identify about six features? This will help you decide between Band 2 and Band 3.		
Has every feature got an example with it? This will help you decide between Band 1 and Band 2.		
Is every example correct? This will help you decide between Band 2 and Band 3.		
Does your partner comment on the effect of each language feature, by telling you something about the feature and what it does ('command sentences make us do something', 'direct address speaks to us directly') rather than making a general comment (such as, 'it keeps the reader reading on')? This will help you decide between Band 1 and Band 2.		
Does your partner explain precisely the effect of the language feature and say something specific about how it might make you feel or respond, or what it makes you think of or imagine? This will help you decide between Band 2 and Band 3.		

Try it yourself

Now it's your turn to attempt a Question 3-style exam task. Read the text and then complete the task below.

Activity 16

Answer the following sample exam question:

3 Now read this text in which Bear Grylls, explorer, author and Chief Scout, writes about the benefits of camping. How does the writer use language features in the text?

Remember to:
- give some examples of language features
- explain the effects. (12 marks)

Bear Grylls,
explorer, author and Chief Scout

Camping brings people together. It also makes for great memories. It doesn't matter whether you're in Kettering or Kathmandu, there's something about spending a night in a tent that restores a sense of peace and simplicity to your life. Pitching a tent is about spending time outdoors, and in summer the world fully comes to life. Seasonal flowers are in bloom, birds are criss-crossing the skies and warm days stretch ahead of you. Somehow everything looks more hopeful when you're peering out of a tent. Going camping doesn't cost much and it doesn't need a lot of planning. Spontaneity is a big part of the appeal.

I think there's a renewed interest in camping at the moment because people want more from life. Camping teaches you things about yourself, it reminds you that we depend on each other and the most precious things in life are friendships, the natural world and reaching our potential. I also think taking children on a camping holiday is one of the most incredible and generous things you can do as a parent.

There's a nice tie between camping, the scouts and the National Trust. The scouting movement began with a camp on beautiful Trust site Brownsea Island in Dorset. Among the peacocks and red squirrels, Baden-Powell set up a camp for 20 young people. Many of these kids were from inner cities and had barely seen a tree before. He got them tracking, fire lighting, stargazing and sailing boats. He opened up a world of new possibilities for such young people, which is what the scouting movement does today. Every year, 400,000 go to camp in Britain's most beautiful places – waking up in tents in the Peak District, the Lake District, the New Forest, you name it. We have a saying in scouting, when it comes to camping: 'Leave nothing behind except your thanks.' It's not just the National Trust's job to look after our landscape. We are all custodians of the world, and the best way to appreciate the countryside is to get out there and enjoy it.

More than 30,000 young people are on scouting waiting lists due to a shortage of adult volunteers. If you love the outdoors and have just two hours to spare a month, you could help. Go to www. scouts.org.uk/join for more details.

What to expect in the exam

In Question 4, you will be asked to compare the **presentational features** of two of the three sources you have already read in the exam.

Presentational features include things that you can see in the sources. We could call these visual devices. Presentational features also include things that help to shape or organize the source. We could call these structural devices.

Question 4 requires you to revisit two out of the three sources, look carefully at them and show that you can:

- identify and describe some of the visual devices of two sources (for example, pictures or interesting fonts) and explain why they may have been chosen

- identify and describe some of the structural devices of two sources (for example, subheadings or bullet points) and explain why they may have been chosen

- compare and contrast the presentational features in the two sources.

Practising the key skills

In the exam, Question 4 may be based on any two of the three sources and is worth 12 marks. A typical Question 4 might look something like this:

What do you understand by this word?

Check the definition of this key term in the box above.

What did you learn about this key term in the Question 3 chapter?

4 Look again at all three sources. Choose two of these sources and compare the way that both texts use presentational features for effect.

Remember to:
- write about the way the texts are presented
- explain the effect of the presentational features
- compare the way they look.

Or Question 4 could look like this:

> **4** Look again at Sources 1 and 3. Compare the way that both texts use presentational features for effect.
>
> Remember to:
> - write about the way the texts are presented
> - explain the effect of the presentational features
> - compare the way they look.

The two types of question

You will notice that there are two possible types of question:

- sometimes you will be asked to choose two sources from the available three

- sometimes you will be told which two sources to write about.

This is because some types of text – for example, biography or autobiography – have no clear presentational features that you could comment on.

At other times, all three sources will have a number of different things to write about and you are free to choose two out of the three to comment on.

You are being asked to do four things in your response to Question 4:

1. Look carefully at two sources.

2. Write about the way they look or have been presented.

3. Suggest some reasons for the choices of presentational features.

4. Compare the way the two sources look.

What are presentational features?

Presentational features are those parts of a text that add to the way it looks – the parts that make a visual impression on a reader. They can also be the things that help it to be more organized – its structure.

Look at the two plans that Students A and B have prepared for a piece of writing describing a beach.

Student (A)

- blue sky/cloudless + blazing sun
- buckets and spades
- melting ice creams
- sea with white-topped waves
- children playing
- beach huts

Student (B)

Student A has used a structural presentational feature (bullet points) to organize his list. Student B has used a visual presentational feature (pictures or doodles) to give clear images of what she intends to write about.

Examples of presentational features might be:

- use of colour
- illustrations or pictures
- different fonts or typefaces
- backgrounds and use of 'white' space
- subheadings
- columns
- photographs
- diagrams
- different font sizes
- headlines/titles
- captions
- bullet points/numbering

> ## Activity 1
> •
> Look back at the leaflet for Brownsea Island on pages 46–47. Which presentational features from the list are used in the leaflet? Make your own list of the features you are able to identify.

Examples of presentational features

Now look carefully at the Mark Scheme for Question 4.

AO2, i, iii English AO3, i, iii English Language	Skills
Band 3 'clear' 'relevant' 9–12 marks	• clear evidence that the texts are understood in relation to presentational features • clear comparison of presentational features • developed comment on the effect of the presentational features in both texts • clear examples of presentational features from both texts
Band 2 'some' 'attempts' 5–8 marks	• some evidence that the texts are understood in relation to presentational features • attempts to compare presentational features • some comment on the effect of presentational features • some examples of presentational features
Band 1 'limited' 1–4 marks	• limited evidence that the texts are understood in relation to presentational feature(s) • simple cross-reference of presentational feature(s) • simple generalized comment on the effect of presentational feature(s) • simple mention of presentational feature(s)

The first rung of the Mark Scheme ladder asks for a 'simple mention of presentational feature(s)', but in order to move up to Bands 2 and 3, you need to provide examples.

Exam tips

Imagine that the examiner can't see the text you are looking at – your first job is to describe clearly what you see.

Giving clear examples

It's easy to say that a news article has photos or headlines – most of them do!

In the exam, to move up the bands, you need to describe more precisely what you see. In other words, you must tell the examiner what is special about the presentation of the text you are dealing with.

Activity 2

1. Look closely at the text opposite and make a list of all the presentational features used in the leaflet.

2. For each feature you have identified in response to question one, write a clear description of what you see, so that you have given the examiner the examples they are looking for.

One has been done for you, below, to help you get started.

Mentions a feature. A Band 1 idea would stop here.

Is now attempting an example. A Band 2 idea would stop here.

The leaflet uses subheadings. 'Events', 'Education' and 'Conferences' are all one type of subheading presented in a crisp, bright, white font. This makes a contrast against the darker background and creates a clear, efficient and organized impression on the reader and suggests that this might be a well-organized and efficient place to hold an educational visit or a conference.

Develops into a clear example and goes on to comment on effect. A Band 3 response would include this much detail.

science has never been this much fun

experiment

Conferences

If you're looking for an unusual conference venue, then look no further. For conferences, business meetings and seminars Catalyst has a range of rooms available including the stunning Observatory gallery for evening corporate events.

Events

Visit during the school holidays and take part in our hands-on workshops and family shows. With an ever changing programme of activities, there's always something new to do.

Education

Catalyst continues to develop its exciting programme of award-winning activities in the education centre. Ranging from KS1 - KS4 we offer everything from hands-on workshops to dynamic shows presented by our own experts or special guest presenters.

develop

Commenting on effects

In the Question 3 chapter, you worked on how to comment on the effects of language. For Question 4 you are also required to comment on effects, but this time on the presentational features you have identified.

Think about the key 'effect' questions; before you make a comment on effect, ask yourself:

How does the presentational feature make you:

- feel?
- behave?
- respond?

What does it make you:

- think of?
- imagine?

Exam tips

Many students write vague statements about the effect of presentational features. The most widely used comment is 'it stands out'.

All presentational features are designed to stand out, so this comment could apply to almost anything. This would be a very 'limited' Band 1 type of comment. Once again, you should be more precise.

Activity 3

Now look at the charity leaflet from Cats Protection opposite. Make a list of all the presentational features you can identify.

I was too little to survive on my own

I was abandoned at three weeks old

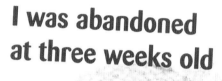

ACTUAL SIZE: 6 inches long

Examples of commenting on effect

Student A has been practising for the exam by writing about the photographs in the leaflet from Cats Protection.

Student A

The leaflet uses photographs of a kitten. The kitten is tiny and very cute in the pictures. It makes you wonder how anyone could have left this little kitten to die. It makes me feel very sad to see this.

Now look at what Student B has written about the photographs in the leaflet:

Student B

A clear and detailed example.

A clear comment on the effect of the photograph – this time on how it makes us feel – including a little analysis of the image itself.

Another clear comment on the effect. This time the student offers us some analysis of the image, commenting on how it makes us feel and how it might make us respond, i.e. by donating to the charity.

The leaflet uses two different photographs of the same tiny kitten. On the cover of the leaflet, the photograph is a close-up of the kitten's face and it seems to be looking directly at us, with big sad eyes. It is sitting outside on a park bench. This gives us the impression the tiny kitten is out in the big wide world, trying to fend for itself. This is designed to make us feel very sorry for the abandoned kitten. Inside the leaflet we have another photograph of the kitten. The second image shows the kitten alongside a ruler, illustrating just how tiny the kitten was when it was found, and is designed to tug on our heart strings. This encourages the reader to donate to the charity so that they can rescue more vulnerable animals.

Activity 4

1. Look at the Mark Scheme on page 55 and identify which skills Student A has demonstrated.

2. What are the key differences between the work that Student A has done and the work that Student B has completed?

Building analytical skills

Analysis involves examining something closely and observing its detail, and then writing that detail down clearly to show how you have understood it. For example, Student A (opposite) wrote a sensible example that showed how he was affected by the photograph. Student B, though, seemed to 'zoom in' on the photographs. Student B provided more details and so was able to show more of her own understanding of the image.

Read the news article below, 'One whale of a tail' and then study the photograph closely.

One whale of a tail

by **Nadia Gilani**

Fluke shot: tourists gape at the sight as a humpback whale's tail fin towers above them.

It was a twist in the tail that was a little too close for comfort.

Tourists were left stunned as a humpback whale's tail fin – known as a fluke – towered out of the water above their flimsy rubber boat.

As it crashed into the ocean the whale watchers' boat threatened to capsize. Luckily, they survived the near miss unharmed.

The moment was captured by tour guide and photographer Tony Beck from another dinghy in the Antarctic Peninsula. 'I've learned to expect the unexpected,' said Mr Beck, 58.

The whale had been feeding on krill when it arched its back and dived out of the water.

'Whenever I see humpback whales doing this I know their tail follows them out of the water. Then poof, it's gone,' said Mr Beck, of Ottawa, Canada.

'It's a real adrenaline rush,' he added.

Key term

Foreground The parts of an image that appear at the very front; the things which seem closest to us.

Background The parts of an image that are at the rear of a photograph and seem farthest away from us or appear behind the text (e.g. in a leaflet).

Activity 5

Working in a small group, discuss the following questions, making notes to help you write a detailed analysis of the photograph below.

1. What do you notice about the landscape in the photograph?

2. How does the snow-covered mountain help us to visualize the size of the whale's tail?

3. Why do you think the whale's tail is placed in the **foreground** of the picture and the boat in the **background**?

4. What do you notice about the colour of the whale's tail compared to the boat?

5. How does the size of the boat compare to the whale's tail?

6. How many people seem to be in the boat?

7. How does the number and size of the people help us to realize the size of the whale's tail?

8. We only see the tail of the whale in this picture – what is suggested about the rest of the whale?

9. How might this make the people in the boat seem vulnerable?

10. What does the picture suggest to you about humans and nature?

Feed back your group's ideas to the class.

Beginning to compare

The third rung of the Mark Scheme ladder on page 55 focuses on how well you are able to compare the presentational features of your two sources. A Band 1 response might make a simple cross-reference, for example:

> Source 1 has a headline but Source 2 doesn't.

To compare means:

- to find things that the sources have in common – the things that are similar
- to find the things that contrast – the things that are different.

In other words, you are linking the presentational features of the two texts.

Two lists of useful linking words are included below.

Words to suggest similarity	Words to suggest difference
by comparison	in contrast
the same as	however
likewise	unlike
in the same way	contrastingly
in common with	on the other hand
similarly	whereas

Activity 6

Look closely at the photograph and caption below.

1. What different impression of the sea do we get from this photograph compared to the photograph on page 61?

2. What impression do we get of the little girl in the photograph?

Child prodi-ski: Isabelle Grinhaff can't even swim yet but is quite comfortable on top of the water. Thought to be Britain's youngest water-skier, she started learning aged two like her father, Marc, of Scotter, Lincolnshire, a former European champion. 'I like going fast,' said the three-year-old, who has her own customized pink skis.

Making comparisons

If we were to compare the photograph above with the one of the whale's tail on page 61, it might be useful to think about it in terms of four key ideas:

- the backgrounds in both photos
- the scale and size of the people in both photos
- the extent to which people are in danger or under threat
- how people look in comparison to the natural world.

Activity 7

In a small group, discuss the four key ideas and complete the table, outlining the key similarities and differences between the photographs.

Similarities and differences	One whale of a tail	Little water skier
The background and landscape		You can only see the sea, which is bluish with white foam on small waves.
The size of the people		
Danger/threat vs. safety/fun		
Nature vs. humans		

Improving an answer

Read this practice answer from Student A, together with the annotations from the Mark Scheme.

Simple cross-reference   *Band 2 example*

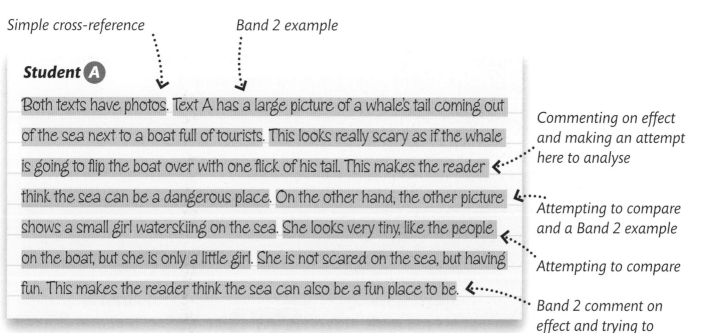

Student A

Both texts have photos. Text A has a large picture of a whale's tail coming out of the sea next to a boat full of tourists. This looks really scary as if the whale is going to flip the boat over with one flick of his tail. This makes the reader think the sea can be a dangerous place. On the other hand, the other picture shows a small girl waterskiing on the sea. She looks very tiny, like the people on the boat, but she is only a little girl. She is not scared on the sea, but having fun. This makes the reader think the sea can also be a fun place to be.

Commenting on effect and making an attempt here to analyse

Attempting to compare and a Band 2 example

Attempting to compare

Band 2 comment on effect and trying to analyse

Activity 8

1. With a partner, discuss three ways you could improve Student A's answer above.

2. Using the notes you collected in Activity 5 and the ideas from your table in Activity 7, rewrite Student A's answer, adding in more detail, more analysis and more interesting comparisons.

Analysing and comparing colours and logos

Many texts use other images such as artwork, symbols or logos as well as, or instead of, photographs.

Colour can be used on many kinds of text and for a variety of presentational features. For example, it can be used for the background of a leaflet, for lettering or in logos and symbols.

Different colours help us to picture different things. They also help to suggest certain moods or feelings. In that way, they can help to create a message for the reader. In other words, colour helps to create a clear effect in the reader's mind.

Look at this striking opening from an unusual love poem:

> When he walked into the party
> With her proudly on his arm
> I saw RED.

Key term

Connotations The pictures we see in our imagination when we think of a particular thing or idea. They are what we might associate with that thing or idea.

Here, we cannot even see a colour, but in our mind's eye, the words create certain **connotations**.

Activity 9

1. What do you think the poet means when she says she 'saw red'?

2. In the spider diagram below, a student has begun to collect some possible connotations of the colour red. Play a game of word-association. How many more connotations of the colour red can you think of?

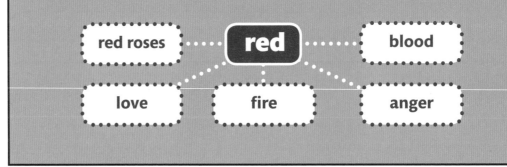

red roses ..... **red** ..... blood

love   fire   anger

Below are three logos from leading charities. They all use colour to help them create a distinct and memorable message.

Activity 10

1. Look at the colour of each logo. What connotations spring to mind for each of these colours?

2. Look closely at the image or picture that makes up the logo:

   a) What is suggested by the green leaf shape?

   b) What associations do you have with the heart shape and the wobbly line – does this remind you of anything?

   c) What does the white candle against the black background suggest?

   d) What does the barbed wire suggest?

3. What kind of work might each of these charities do? Give reasons for your ideas.

4. Choose two of the logos. Write a paragraph comparing them.

   Remember to:

   - *describe* each logo in detail

   - comment on the *connotations* of the different colours

   - comment on the *connotations* of the different pictures

   - *compare* the logos by discussing the differences between them

   - *explain* how you think a reader might be affected by the message each logo creates.

Many students write about bold font in their work, but don't look at the size or shape of the lettering. This can sometimes have important or interesting clues that link to the text itself, its purpose or its audience. Check your two chosen sources for different font types and look at them closely to see if you can make any suggestions about their choice.

Analysing font styles

Different fonts or typefaces can conjure up different ideas or impressions in your mind's eye. Certain types of lettering can fit with certain themes. By 'zooming in' carefully on different fonts and thinking about what they suggest to you, you can add another dimension to your comparative Question 4 answer.

Activity 11

The designer has mixed up the font styles for the magazine titles below.

1. Discuss with a partner why each title looks strange.

2. Suggest which font style belongs with which magazine and why.

A The Gothic Horror Fanzine

B Computer Scientists' Monthly

C The Journal of Classic Poetry

D The Primary School Teachers' Review

Building a comparative response

When you are putting together an answer for Question 4 you should begin by following these clear steps:

- Look closely at the two sources you have chosen or been given.

- Identify no more than three or four key aspects of presentation that you can compare or contrast; for example, use of colours, logos and photographs.

- Make notes or a plan of the features you are able to compare or contrast.

Look closely at the two texts connected with the charity Help for Heroes (below and on page 70).

Source 1

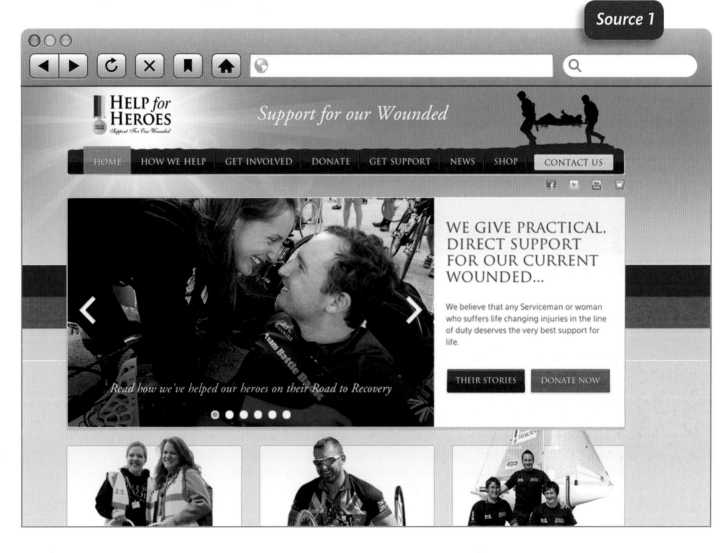

News > UK News > Military

Help for Heroes new rehab centre: 'This is a launchpad for life'

Charity's flagship recovery centre in Wiltshire has all the facilities to help injured soldiers – and could even provide the next crop of Paralympic gold medallists for Rio 2016

Amputee Steve Arnold uses a hand bike in the new Help for Heroes centre at Tedworth House.

Exactly three years ago Sergeant Simon Harmer was a month into a tour of Afghanistan when he stepped on a roadside bomb during a routine patrol. His right leg was blown off and his left leg had to be amputated back at camp.

On Thursday however, 36-year-old Harmer was taking a tour of state-of-the-art facilities at the Help For Heroes flagship recovery centre in Wiltshire and dreaming of sporting glory. 'I want to try to become a Paralympian,' he said.

'My swimming is pretty good at the moment – I'm beating able-bodied competitors. But it could be cycling or canoeing. I'm definitely going to give it a go. I don't want to look back in 20 years' time and regret not having tried it. I'm excited beyond words at this place. They're going to struggle to get me out of the door.'

The tour was the first glimpse of the new facilities at Tedworth House in Tidworth, one of the charity's four UK recovery centres due to fully open next year and set to care for and inspire injured service personnel for the next century.

Planning your comparison

Look at Student A's plan below which compares the presentational features of the texts on pages 69 and 70.

Help for Heroes webpage	Online news article
Uses lots of colour – red, white and blue, which reminds me of the union flag and is very patriotic	Mainly black and white but with bits of red on the tabs for 'Military' Photo is in colour and there are some bits of red/white and blue on the guys' T-shirts
Uses an image of two soldiers carrying a wounded soldier on a stretcher – very emotive – blue sky/moonlight? Hope?	Uses a photo of real injured soldiers. Amazing picture of soldiers with no legs cycling. Picture is blurred, which suggests they are moving fast
Uses a logo like a medal for bravery The slogan: 'Support for our Wounded' seems important and suggests pride	No logos used here but headlines and captions Quotations included Gives a summary

Activity 12

1. Talk about this plan with a partner, looking closely at the presentational features on the Help for Heroes webpage and the online news article. What interesting things has Student A noted?

2. Discuss the different effects that each of the presentational features identified in the plan have on you.

Remember your key questions:

How does it make me:

- feel?

- behave?

- respond?

What does it make me:

- think of?

- imagine?

Analysing an answer

Student A has decided that the most important aspect of both texts is the visual images and begins his answer like this:

Detailed description of the image

Clear and interesting comment on effect

Student A

Source 1 has a silhouette image of two soldiers carrying a wounded soldier on a stretcher. This is a drawing and not a photograph, so does not identify anyone specifically. This suggests that all soldiers are vulnerable and any one of them could be injured when they are on duty. The soldiers are against a background of a midnight blue sky but there are rays of moonlight behind them lighting their way. This might suggest hope for the wounded and links to the idea of helping heroes of battle.

In contrast, Source 2 uses a photograph of real people who have benefited from the Help for Heroes charity. We see Sergeant Harmer and his colleague training hard on bicycles powered by their hands. The photograph is very dramatic because the soldiers have no legs. They are moving at a great speed because their hands are almost a blur. This is very inspiring and helps you to see the benefit of the charity's work.

The colours on the webpage ...

More detail and clarity about the image

A second very sensible comment on effect

Uses a clear comparison

Detailed description of the photograph – very clear

Offers some analysis of the photograph

Sensible comment on effect

In Question 4, it is always better to choose about three presentational features and write about them in detail, rather than write about everything in a sketchy, limited way.

Activity 13

Continue Student A's response beginning, 'The colours on the webpage ...'.

- Use the paragraphs opposite as your Band 3 guide.
- Use the notes in the plan on page 71.
- Use your own ideas.

You should try to:

- describe each presentational feature in detail
- comment on the connotations or associations of the colours in both texts
- comment on the connotations or associations of the logo
- compare the differences in the use of headline/caption in both texts
- link to the slogan in the logo
- explain how you think a reader might be affected by the message each of the features creates or how you are affected yourself.

Use the notes in the plan on page 71.

Exam tips

Spend some time looking closely for a few interesting things that you feel confident to write about in detail.

Students who try to write about everything tend to make simple, generalized comments such as, 'Source 1 has a photo and so does Source 2. Source 1 has a headline, but Source 2 doesn't.'

HELP *for* **HEROES**   *Support for our Wounded*

Try it yourself

Now it's your turn to practise all your Question 4 skills. Try Activity 14 below.

Activity 14

Answer the following sample exam question.

4 Look at the two information leaflets for visitor attractions on pages 76 and 77. Compare the way both texts use presentational features for effect.

Remember to:

- write about the way the texts are presented
- explain the effect of the presentational features
- compare the way they look. (12 marks)

Remember to:

- identify about three examples of presentational features to compare or contrast between the two texts – choose the ones you feel most confident with

- write up your examples in detail

- accompany each description with a clear explanation of the effect of the feature, thinking about how it makes you respond, behave, think or feel, or what it makes you imagine

- link your feature in Source 1 to Source 2 by writing about what is similar or what is different

- write up your points in crisp, clear Standard English.

Self-assessment

When you have finished your answer, use this student-friendly version of the Mark Scheme to help you check your progress.

AO2, i, iii English AO3, i, iii English Language	Skills
Band 3 'clear' 'relevant' 9–12 marks	• I have made a clear comparison of presentational features by making sensible and thoughtful links between them so that my answer feels clear and organized. • I have made clear comments on the effect of the presentational features in both texts by thinking about how readers might respond to them or how I might respond. • I have written clear and detailed examples of presentational features from both texts, perhaps with some analysis.
Band 2 'some' 'attempts' 5–8 marks	• I have attempted to compare presentational features using linking words for some of the examples I have chosen. • I have made some comment on the effect of presentational features by thinking about what the colours might mean or whether the places look appealing. • I have given some examples of presentational features by describing, for example, different background colours, fonts and photographs.
Band 1 'limited' 1–4 marks	• I have made a simple cross-reference of presentational feature(s) by saying something like 'Source 1 uses colour and so does Source 2'. • I have made simple generalized comments on the effect of presentational feature(s) like 'It stands out'. • I have mentioned a presentational feature(s), e.g. colour or picture.

spaceport

3,2,1...
WE HAVE LIFT OFF!

Imagine a whole galaxy under one roof, where learning about space has never been so much fun.

With star filled attractions and exhibitions light years beyond Earth, ride the supersonic space simulator, take a seat in our 360° space dome planetarium, become a stargazer in the Milky Way and enjoy out of this world events.

WE CONSTANTLY MOVE THROUGH **SPACE** AT A RATE OF **530KM A SECOND!**

...IF YOU DON'T KNOW IT, YOU HAVEN'T BEEN

ASTRONAUTS CAN'T BURP IN **SPACE!**

SPACE DOME PLANETARIUM
Experience life as an astronaut and take a 360° journey through space in the amazing planetarium.

EXPLORER SIMULATOR
Blast off to the stars in this amazing ride - and see just how it feels to be a real space explorer!

GET LOST IN SPACE
Enter through a worm hole and get hands on with our interactive exhibitions as you travel through space.

THE FINAL FRONTIER
Stock up on your space supplies with a variety of, books, toys and exciting space themed souvenirs.

THE AVERAGE DISTANCE OF THE **EARTH** FROM THE **SUN** IS ABOUT **93 MILLION MILES!**

Source 2

So many wild days...

Unforgettable wildlife encounters await. Explore an exciting mix of wetlands and woodlands on foot, by boat, or canoe. From bustling play areas to secluded wildlife havens – take time to discover, watch, learn or play.

...a day to watch wildlife

» Flocks of migrating **pink-footed geese**.
» Thousands of wintering **whooper swans**.
» Thriving **reedbeds, meadows & woodlands**.
» Join our **daily guided walks** and **talks**.
» Marvel at the sight of **daily** winter **swan feeds**.

...a day of adventures

» Pick up a paddle on a **canoe safari**.*
» Sit back and relax on a guided **boat tour**.*
» Splash & dash in our **new adventure play area**.
» Let your creativity run wild **building a den**.
» Step into the past at the **neolithic Mere Tun**.

...a day to get closer

» Don't miss the **Downy Duckling Experience**.
» Discover mini-beasts at the **pond zones**.
» Watch **otters** & **beavers** during expert talks.
» **Meet exotic birds** from all over the world.

What kind of day will you choose?

New for 2012

...so visit today

For a new experience each visit, check **wwt.org.uk/martinmere** for **daily activities** and **special events throughout the year**, or call us on 01704 895181.

*Canoe & boat safaris are only available at certain times of the year. Additional charges apply. Children over 5 only.

Preparing for Section B: Writing

What is the content and focus of the exam?

Unit 1 Section B is worth 40 marks. It is where you are the writer and your ability to produce non-fiction texts is assessed. You have to complete two writing tasks: one shorter task worth 16 marks and one longer task worth 24 marks. In the shorter task you have to write to inform/explain/describe and in the longer task you have to write to argue/persuade. You have to show that you can match your style of writing to fit the topic, purpose and audience.

How to use your time in the exam

You should aim to spend 1 hour on the Writing section (having spent 1 hour 15 minutes on the Reading section). The following provides a suggestion for how you could divide up your time in the Writing section of the exam:

Question and word count	Marks available	Suggested timing
Question 5: There is no specified length, but you should aim to write about a page of your answer booklet for Question 5.	16 marks (10 marks for Communication and Organization of Ideas; 6 marks for Accuracy)	25 minutes (including a few minutes at the start to plan and a few minutes to proofread your answer at the end)
Question 6: There is no specified length, but you should aim to write about two pages of your answer booklet for Question 6.	24 marks (16 marks for Communication and Organization of Ideas; 8 marks for Accuracy)	35 minutes (including a few minutes at the start to plan and a few minutes to proofread your answer at the end)

While both questions test the same skills, you are expected to develop your ideas more in the longer task. This Writing section is therefore divided into two chapters, with each one focusing on a separate question. It is essential that you attempt both Writing questions in the exam in order to demonstrate all the necessary skills. If you miss out a question, you will not achieve the mark that you want.

Assessment Objectives (AOs)

Assessment Objectives are the skills being assessed during your GCSE course. Below is a list that shows you the AOs that you need to demonstrate in the Writing section of the Unit 1 exam:

AO number	AO wording	Question this AO applies to in Section B: Writing
AO3, i English AO4, i English Language	Write to communicate clearly, effectively and imaginatively, using and adapting forms and selecting vocabulary appropriate to task and purpose in ways that engage the reader.	You need to demonstrate this AO in Question 5 and Question 6 (Communication).
AO3, ii English AO4, ii English Language	Organize information and ideas into structured and sequenced sentences, paragraphs and whole texts, using a variety of linguistic and structural features to support cohesion and overall coherence.	You need to demonstrate this AO in Question 5 and Question 6 (Organization of Ideas).
AO3, iii English AO4, iii English Language	Use a range of sentence structures for clarity, purpose and effect, with accurate punctuation and spelling.	You need to demonstrate this AO in Question 5 and Question 6 (Accuracy).

By working through the following Writing chapters, you will practise these key skills and learn exactly where you need to demonstrate them in the exam in order to achieve your best possible mark.

Mark Scheme

The examiner uses a Mark Scheme to assess your responses. There are three main mark bands in the Mark Scheme for Foundation Tier: Band 1, Band 2 and Band 3.

Each mark band is summed up by a key word or words. For Writing, the key words are:

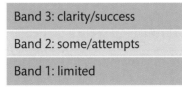

Band 3: clarity/success

Band 2: some/attempts

Band 1: limited

Each mark band consists of a range of skills, based on the Assessment Objectives above, which you have to demonstrate – if you imagine the skills inside the bands as rungs on a ladder, the further up the ladder you climb, the more demanding the skills become. This book aims to help you develop those skills to achieve the best mark of which you are capable.

The key words and the skills being tested are the same for both Writing questions, and extracts from the Mark Scheme that examiners use are included in both chapters.

Writing Question 5

What to expect in the exam

In the exam, you will be asked to complete two writing tasks. Question 5 is a short writing task, but is worth 16 marks in total.

You can earn up to 10 marks for the way you organize your writing and communicate your ideas to your reader. This includes:

- using paragraphs or other interesting ways to organize your writing – for example, sections in a leaflet or addresses in a letter
- choosing the right kind of interesting vocabulary
- making good choices of language special effects – like the ones you learned about in the Question 3 chapter – for the task you have been given.

You can also earn up to six marks for how accurate your writing is. This includes:

- showing that you can write in Standard English
- punctuating your work accurately
- spelling as many words correctly as you can
- using interesting types of sentence.

A typical Question 5 might look something like one of the following:

> **5** Write a short article for your college magazine, informing students about a charity event you are organizing.

> **5** Write a letter to your local newspaper, explaining why young people need more things to do in your area.

> **5** Write a feature article for a travel magazine, describing a good place for a family to visit in a half-term holiday.

Purpose, audience and form

You will not get a choice of task in the exam, so it is important to read the task carefully and work out precisely what you are being asked to do. The safest way to do that is to stop, think and note down the following three things:

- What job is my piece of writing going to do? What is its **purpose**?

- Who am I supposed to be writing this for? Who is my imaginary **audience**?

- How should my text be set out? If this was a professional piece of writing, how would it look and what **form** would it take?

The **purpose** is the 'job' your piece of writing is doing – the question will tell you this. Question 5 focuses on three purposes of writing: to describe, inform or explain. Your question will give you one of these three to focus on.

The **audience** is the person or people you are writing for – the question will either tell or suggest this to you. You may be asked to write, for example, for readers of a local newspaper or students in your school or college.

The **form** is the type of response you are producing – the question will tell you what it should be. You may be asked, for example, to write a letter, an article, a blog entry or a leaflet.

Activity 1

Look at the three example questions opposite and for each one, consider:

a) What is the purpose?

b) Who is the audience? Who are you writing for? Is this always completely clear or do you have to sometimes work it out? What clues can you use to help you?

c) What is the form? How should your text look on the page? Have you ever seen any real texts similar to the ones in the question?

Mark Scheme

This is the Mark Scheme that is used to mark the content and organization of your work for Question 5.

AO3, i, ii English AO4, i, ii English Language	Skills
Band 3 'clarity' 'success' 9–10 marks	**Content** • shows clarity of thought and communicates with success • engages the reader with more detail for purpose • clearly communicates the purpose • writes in a register which is clearly appropriate for audience • uses linguistic features appropriate to purpose • uses vocabulary effectively, including discursive markers **Organization** • uses paragraphs effectively in the whole text • uses a variety of structural features
Band 2 'some' 'attempts' 5–8 marks	**Content** • communicates ideas with some success • engages the reader with some detail for purpose • shows some awareness of the purpose • attempts to write in a register which is appropriate for audience • uses some linguistic features appropriate to purpose • attempts to vary vocabulary and use discursive markers **Organization** • uses paragraphs, which may be tabloid, at times correctly placed • some evidence of structural features
Band 1 'limited' 1–4 marks	**Content** • communicates with limited success • reference to one or two ideas linked to task • limited awareness of the purpose • limited awareness of the appropriate register for audience • simple use of linguistic feature(s) • uses simple vocabulary **Organization** • random or no paragraphs • limited use of structural features

At first, this seems complicated, but it is just a ladder of skills like the ones you saw in the chapters on Reading. The skills listed in the right-hand column show you exactly what the examiner is looking for.

Checklist for success for Question 5

Below is a checklist of the types of questions examiners will ask themselves when marking your Question 5 answer. You could use a checklist like this to reflect on your writing.

1. Are you organizing your work in paragraphs to show where the topic changes in your writing? ☑

   and/or

2. Are you using some of the layout features you might find in a real text of this kind? ☑

3. Are you using a good vocabulary? ☐

4. Have you remembered who you are supposed to be writing for and made it sound right for them? ☐

5. Have you used the right kinds of language features for this purpose? ☐

6. Are you really sure about the purpose and have you stuck to it all the way through? ☐

7. Have you used some details to make your writing interesting to read? ☐

8. Is your piece of writing clear from beginning to end? Can it be read all the way through without the examiner having to stop and double-check what is being said? ☐

Getting your work organized

For Question 5, you have 25 minutes to complete your task. This means you have to work quickly and efficiently.

You are advised on the exam paper to 'try to write about a page'.

Think about the form you have been asked to write in and make a decision about how you will organize your writing.

Organizational devices

In the box below is a list of some of the different things you can use to organize your work.

paragraphs	headlines	subheadings
written sections in boxes		address set to the right
columns	bullet pointed or numbered sections	
Dear ...	yours sincerely or faithfully	
captions	menu bars	

Different types of text use different organizational devices to make their content clear for the reader. For example, a letter looks very different to a newspaper article and includes different devices.

Activity 2

Look at each of the forms in the table and decide what organizational devices you could use to help you organize your writing most successfully to look like 'the real thing'. Use the list opposite to help you, along with your own ideas.

Form	Organizational devices you would use
Newspaper article	
Letter	
Webpage	
Leaflet	
Magazine feature	

Exam tips

Always spend some time thinking about the structure of your work. If you are asked to write a letter, make it look like a real letter with addresses and 'Dear …', plus a sign-off like 'Yours sincerely' or 'Best wishes', as well as paragraphs in the main text.

If you are asked to write an article, give it a headline and perhaps a subheading as well as writing in paragraphs. That way, you will always move up from Band 1 for structure and organization.

Planning your content

It may seem unrealistic to sit and write a plan for a 25-minute task, but jotting down your key ideas as you are reading and thinking about form, purpose and audience will help you to stay on-task and remain focused.

In one page, you might realistically write three or four paragraphs of a letter or article, or four or five sections of a leaflet or webpage. You need to think about what points and ideas you will include in your writing.

You could:

- create a brief spider diagram
- list your ideas
- make a flow chart.

Sample plans

You can create a plan in whatever style suits you best; for example, a simple list, a flow chart or a diagram. Look at the plans that Students A and B have written for the following example task.

5 Write a letter to your local newspaper, explaining why young people in your area need more things to do.

Student A

Too many unhealthy teens sitting at home on computer/TV, etc.

No safe places to go in the evening/kids hanging around on streets

Problem

Kids become bored and might cause problems or be tempted into bad behaviour/vandalism/drugs

Sports facilities – how these will help...

Revision clubs – how these will help...

Solution

Youth club – how this will help...

Student **B**

- Too many unhealthy teens sitting at home on computer/TV, etc.

- No safe places to go in the evening/kids hanging around on streets

- Kids become bored and might cause problems or be tempted into bad behaviour/vandalism/drugs

- Finish with some suggestions – youth club/sports facilities/revision clubs – explain how these will all help young people and the town

- Remember to structure as a letter: 'Dear Sir,' etc.

Activity 3

Choose a planning style and create a brief plan for one of the other example questions on page 80.

Even if you just spend two or three minutes planning, aim to work out how your piece of writing might end. Note down how it will be structured. This will give you a clear focus.

Boosting your vocabulary

In the exam, you only have a limited time to show off your skills. You have to remember that you are trying to show your 'best side' – a clear snapshot of what you can do.

A good way to do this is by showing off your best and most ambitious vocabulary. In the exam, the content mark is higher than the accuracy mark. It is always better to include adventurous vocabulary, even if you are unsure of how to spell some of the words you choose. Just try your best with your spelling. For Band 2 an examiner would expect to see some complex spellings, but not all of them correct. Band 3 would require more accuracy, however.

Exam tips

Read anything and everything. It's the only way to keep adding to your store of new words. Think of new words like treasure: when you read or hear a new one, look it up in a dictionary. If you have Internet access, you can find out its meaning in a few seconds.

Activity 4

Below is an extract from a text about an exploration the writer did in the Arctic, where she came face to face with a polar bear.

Read the extract below, which has had much of its exciting vocabulary removed. With a partner, suggest words of your own which might fit into the gaps.

The _____ snow-covered wilderness opens up before me, _____, a place that few have seen or will ever _____ to.

The coastline _____ out of the frost-tipped waters, a _____ _____ mass of white against the pastel blue and pink edged skies as the morning _____ into a short afternoon.

This is a place of almost dazzling beauty but also of terrifying dangers, where _____ of death-trap ice remind us of our _____.

This is a place where magical creatures can step through the _____, frozen fog of this _____ land and we watch amazed, frozen to the spot now by more than just the _____ cold.

From beyond the _____, a _____ _____ is on the _____.

Across the _____ of powder she _____, at first as small as a _____, then gradually emerging as a _____ _____.

And yet, as she gazed out towards our ship, not more than 20 metres from the shore, her eyes, _____, studied me _____ for what seemed like an age and I knew I had nothing to fear from her.

Activity 5

1. Working in a small group, look at the vocabulary bank below. Use dictionaries to find out the meanings of any words you are unsure about.

2. In pairs, try to work out which words and phrases from the vocabulary bank the writer originally chose to fit into each space in the text.

3. Then discuss and make notes on the following:

   a) How do words like 'looms', 'fades', 'prowl' and 'padded' give an interesting sense of movement in the text?

   b) How does the phrase 'endless and inhospitable' make us feel about the place the writer describes?

   c) What is interesting about the way the writer describes the polar bear? Can you identify three different words or phrases to describe the bear? Do they all give the same impression?

4. Working on your own, choose four words or phrases from the vocabulary bank. Use these to write an opening paragraph describing a different place.

looms	fades	padded
endless and inhospitable	weirdly surreal	impassively
prowl	vulnerable limitations	fearful predator
ephemeral	gulf	jagged crests
	mass of vanilla fur	jet black
	favourite teddy bear	vast
		venture
		floating shards
		remote
		numbing

Choosing the right voice

For every task you complete, bear in mind who your audience would be. For example, have you been asked to write to your local MP or for students? Just as in conversation, where we may speak differently in different situations and with different people, we might use different types of language when we write for different types of people.

The right 'voice' to suit an audience is called the register. You will see this word in the Mark Scheme on page 82. The right register is created by:

- your choice of vocabulary
- your choice of language features
- the tone in which you write.

What is tone?

When we speak to people we use different tones all the time. Our tone of voice indicates, for example, if we are being polite, grumpy, interested or angry.

In writing, we still create a tone of voice by the way we address our audience and how formal or informal we are when we communicate with them.

How formal or informal writing is can sometimes be difficult to pinpoint. It is useful to think of some spoken situations and then make some comparisons.

Activity 6

Look at the following spoken situations and think about the kinds of talk that would take place in each.

Highly formal	Formal	Informal	Highly informal
Being on a jury in a courtroom	Taking part in a job interview	Going out for a pizza with friends or family	Chatting to your best friend on the phone

Activity 7

Now look at these examples of written texts. Suggest two more text types that you think would fall under each register heading.

Highly formal	Formal	Informal	Highly informal
Legal documents	Job application letter	Film or music gig review	Text message to a friend
Contracts	Broadsheet news article on serious topic like politics		

Whether you are writing formally or informally, however, you will still use **Standard English**. Being informal does not mean that you do not follow the rules of Standard English. It just means you may be more friendly or open in your approach, perhaps using a little humour.

For example, if you were writing a revision guide for students, you might begin:

> Hey guys, it's that dreaded time of year again. The exams are looming and it's time to get down to some serious revision.

Key term

Standard English The version of English that uses the vocabulary, sentence structures and spellings that we all generally agree to be the correct ones.

Exam tips

In your exam, you are likely to be given tasks that require you to write formally or informally, never highly formally or highly informally. You have to make a choice when you think about who your audience might be.

Writing for a purpose

In Question 5 you will be asked to complete a short piece of writing to: inform or explain or describe.

These words describe the purpose of your piece of writing (the job it has to do).

The examples below are all about the same topic – a holiday to a Greek island – but they are written with different purposes in mind.

1 Turquoise-blue sea meeting an expanse of blue sky is what I see from my balcony. Crickets chirp in the wild thyme bushes whose scent wafts from the olive grove below. The gentle warmth of the Kefalonia sunshine surrounds me. Dotted on the hillside is a ramshackle collection of tiny white farmhouses and pink-roofed villas.

2 Kefalonia is a small island off the west coast of Greece. It is only a few miles wide but has at least 50 beaches. Some of these beaches are special sites where turtles come to lay their eggs and are therefore protected.

The island is also a big producer of olive oil and very good wines.

3 After a cold, long winter, we decided to take a well-earned break to Kefalonia. We all needed some sunshine and a place where we could just relax. Because our last few holidays had been spent camping in the UK, where the rain clouds were never far away, we decided to save up and go abroad. As a result, we stepped off the plane on a July day into the kind of heat that feels like a warm bath.

Activity 8

1. Try to identify which of the pieces of writing is doing the following things:

   a) telling us facts and figures, giving us the main ideas about the place (*informing* you about the island holiday)

   b) giving reasons for the visit, why or how the holiday took place (*explaining* why the holiday took place)

   c) using language features to make you imagine or picture the place in your mind's eye (*describing* the place and the experience).

2. Discuss the differences.

The top informers

Below is a list of the key language features used when writing to inform.

- **facts**
- **opinions**
- **statistics**
- statement sentences
- **proper nouns**

- lists
- **adjectives** to give a precise picture
- technical or **subject-specific words**

Writing to inform means that you are going to tell your reader about something – clear statement sentences will help you do that.

Present information to your reader in a way that is clear so that they have more knowledge about it when they have finished reading your piece of work. Be factual and support your knowledge with statistics or subject-specific words.

Write in a way that is factual and logical, but not boring! Use adjectives and lists to add variety as well as more precise information.

Write in a fair and balanced way so that your reader can trust the knowledge you are giving them. Keep your opinions fair.

Exam tips

Think back to your work on language in the Question 3 chapter. The key language features you are expected to identify in the source material in the Reading section of the exam are the kinds of language features you will need to include in your writing.

Key term

Fact Something which can be proven and which we know to be true.

Opinion A viewpoint that someone holds. Opinions can sometimes seem like facts if presented convincingly enough.

Statistic The use of numbers or figures.

Proper noun A word or words which name something specific, such as people, places, days, months, titles of books, plays and films. All proper nouns begin with a capital letter. Your name is a proper noun.

Adjective A describing word.

Subject-specific words The use of a collection of words or phrases which link to a particular topic; for example, 'software', 'hard drive' and 'megabyte' are specific to the subject of computing.

Dahl uses statement sentences and gives us names and a date. How does this help you as a reader?

How do adjectives like 'old', 'paint peeling' and 'vibrating' give you more precise information about the ship? What do they tell you?

Dahl uses facts and statistics as well as some technical terms about the ship he was on. How does this help us to picture the ship?

Dahl uses place names (proper nouns) and listing here. What is he trying to communicate to us?

From *Going Solo* by Roald Dahl

The ship that was carrying me away from England to Africa in the autumn of 1938 was called the *SS Mantola*. She was an old paint-peeling tub of 9,000 tons with a single tall funnel and a vibrating engine that rattled the tea-cups in their saucers on the dining-room tables.

The voyage from Port of London to Mombasa would take two weeks and on the way we were going to call in at Marseilles, Malta, Port Said, Suez, Port Sudan and Aden. Nowadays you can fly to Mombasa in a few hours and you stop nowhere and nothing is fabulous any more, but in 1938 a journey like that was full of stepping-stones and East Africa was a long way from home, especially if your contract with the Shell Company said you were to stay there for three years at a stretch. I was twenty-two when I left. I would be twenty-five before I saw my family again.

Dahl gives his opinion here on the journey now compared to then. How does his opinion help us to understand more about his journey at the time?

Dahl uses numbers again here but to indicate time. Why do you think he mentions these precise ages?

To inform us, Dahl uses:

- facts
- opinions
- statement sentences
- proper nouns (names of places and the ship)
- lists
- adjectives
- technical references.

Before you begin on an informative writing task, you need to work out just what kinds of things your reader *needs* to know and what they might *want* to know.

If you were tackling the question below, you would need to consider the kinds of things the students in your school or college would need to know about your charity event.

> **5** Write a short leaflet for your college magazine, informing students about a charity event you are organizing.

Student A has put together some notes in order to practise the question above. He has been thinking about what the audience needs to know and what they might want to know.

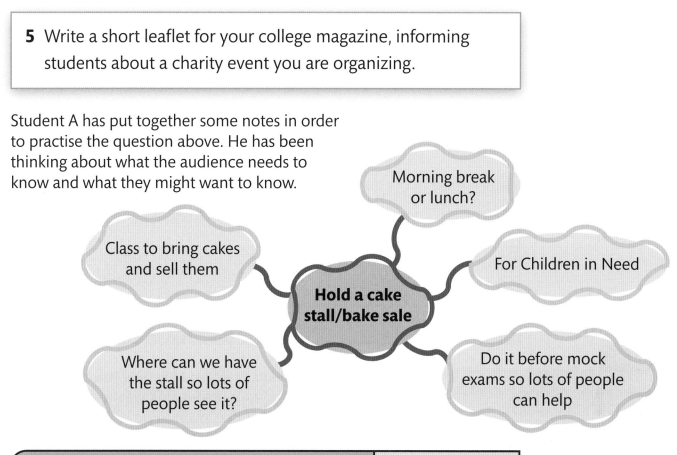

Morning break or lunch?

Class to bring cakes and sell them

For Children in Need

Hold a cake stall/bake sale

Where can we have the stall so lots of people see it?

Do it before mock exams so lots of people can help

Activity 10 **Peer-assessment**

1. Using Student A's notes, write the opening paragraph of the leaflet about the charity event. Include as many of the techniques Roald Dahl has used in the passage on page 94 as you can.

2. Swap your work with a partner. Examine your partner's opening paragraph and note down:

  a) how many of the key techniques to inform you can find

  b) any information about the event that is missing.

3. Suggest one further piece of information you might want about this event.

4. Discuss your feedback with your partner.

The top describers

Below is a list of the key language features used when writing to describe.

- interesting **verbs** and **adverbs**
- adjectives
- **noun phrases**
- metaphor and simile
- using the senses
- personification
- onomatopoeia
- alliteration
- listing
- **repetition**

Activity 11

How many of the key language features listed above do you know? Test yourself to see if you can remember definitions for:

a) metaphor **b)** simile **c)** onomatopoeia

d) alliteration **e)** personification.

When you have finished, check the definitions on page 39 to see how many you got right.

Key term

Verb An action or doing word, e.g. laughing, hop, sleep.

Adverb A word that tells us how a verb is carried out, e.g. happily, slowly, angrily. Adverbs often end in -ly.

Noun phrase A group of words that include a noun and a pronoun and/or adjective, e.g. the scary dog.

Repetition When a word or phrase is included more than once in a text.

Writing to describe means that you are going to create a picture of something for your reader. You will need those clear statement sentences once again to do that, but you can also create interesting patterns in descriptive pieces using listing or repetition.

You are going to create a picture or a visual image for your reader in a way that is clear so that they see it for themselves when they have finished reading your work. So, be creative and make the picture vivid by using adjectives or noun phrases. Help your reader to make comparisons so they can imagine more clearly by using metaphors and similes.

You need to write in a way that is appealing to the senses, but you don't have to trawl through sight, sound, smell, taste and touch! Using senses occasionally can add variety, and 'sound effects' like onomatopoeia and alliteration can add to the experience for your reader.

Read this extract from a book about things to do in the outdoors. It describes winter.

Winter

Winter can be bleak, no doubt about it, but it can also be stunningly beautiful. The sharp air seems cleaner somehow and one feels truly alive when the air is biting. Free of foliage, skies are huge and empty and it's far easier to spot wildlife that is still up and about. On frosty mornings, landscapes glitter and the ground's deliciously crunchy underfoot. Winter is an excuse to wear thick socks and ridiculous hats and to warm up after bracing walks with hot chocolate and buttered crumpets. It's a wonderful time to make plans for your garden, to help winter wildlife and to indulge in some serious armchair bird watching after baking a bird cake.

The frozen months can be especially tough for wildlife. Days are short and for many creatures, especially small birds, finding enough food to survive takes up almost every hour of daylight. The winter solstice on 21 December marks the shortest day. After this the days do get longer, though the coldest winter weather and highest chance of snow is often in January and February.

Winter wildlife watching opportunities are many, however. Trees have lost their leaves and it's possible to see the shape of their trunks and branches in vivid detail and to spot wildlife sheltering in them more clearly. Winter is great for bird watching, as long as you wrap up warm. Large numbers of migratory ducks, geese and swans are around, and other winter visitors to look for include redwing, fieldfare and sometimes waxwing.

Listen for tawny owls hooting, as they begin their courtship displays in winter. Tawny owls are at their noisiest from December onwards.

Activity 12

1. Collect examples of the different techniques the writer uses to describe winter on page 97 in a table like the one below.

2. Then, work with a partner to collect ideas to describe summer. Complete the third column of the table.

3. On your own, write two or three paragraphs describing a perfect summer. Use as many of the examples of the techniques you collected in your table as possible.

4. Share your response with your partner and identify any areas where you might improve on your description.

Describing techniques	Winter	Summer
Adjectives		hazy
Noun phrases	The sharp air	The humid air
Personification		
Interesting verbs		basking
Alliteration		
Listing	Redwing, fieldfare and sometimes waxwing	
Onomatopoeia		

Key term

Anecdote A mini-story about someone's life or experiences that is shared with the reader.

Direct address When a writer uses the word 'you' as if they were speaking directly to the reader; for example, 'You will understand how I felt when I got that special letter.'

The top explainers

Below is a list of the key language features used when writing to explain.

- using reasoning
- facts
- personal opinions and feelings
- statement sentences
- using comparisons
- repetition
- **anecdotes**
- involving the reader through **direct address**

Writing to explain means that you are going to share something with your reader, so involve them in your piece of work, perhaps using direct address.

Present your reasons for something to your reader in a way that is clear, so that they have more of an understanding about it when they have finished reading. You could make a comparison, repeat key ideas or share an anecdote.

Again, write in a way that is factual and logical, but it may include more personal details or references to feelings.

Your reader needs to have all of their questions answered about the topic, so stick to clear statement sentences.

Before you begin, work out just what kinds of things need to be shared and what you want your reader to understand.

Explanation markers and connectives

Explanations are often about sharing personal experiences or viewpoints, but you need to give reasons for your thoughts or actions and to do that you need to use a special kind of language feature. We will call these explanation markers and explanation connectives.

These special features give a signal to your reader that you are about to show them your reasoning. Explanation markers are used at the beginning of a sentence to do this and explanation connectives part of the way through a sentence to join one idea to another.

Exam tips

Concentrate on using the right kinds of markers and connectives to ensure you are explaining and not just telling or narrating.

Explanation markers	Explanation connectives
One cause of...	if...
The reason...	when...
Consequently...	so...
The consequences of...	because...
The main factor...	as a result...
I realized that...	which leads to...

Activity 13

Work in pairs to complete the task below. You need to link the ideas by adding connectives or markers to build a detailed explanation. Try to use two or three markers and/or connectives to link each pairing. An example has been done to get you started.

a) We need to recycle our litter ... we will all end up polluting our environment.

> We need to recycle our litter <u>because</u> if you throw things away, they are no longer any use. <u>As a result</u>, they just end up in a landfill site, <u>which leads</u> to them damaging the environment. <u>The consequence</u> of us not recycling is that we produce so much waste it's impossible to get rid of it. <u>As a result</u>, we will all end up polluting our environment.

b) Revising is very important ... this will help you feel confident on the day of the exam.

c) Taking up a sport can change your life ... you will make friends too.

Considering a student response

Activity 14

Look at the sample question below and then read Student A's response opposite. Using the Mark Scheme on page 82, decide what mark this piece of work would get for content and organization.

A general topic – choose something personal to you

How can you make your piece appealing to, say, 14- to 24-year-olds?

Timing – needs to be crisp and well organized

Two parts to think about here – which one will you have more to say about?

5 A student website is running a feature on hobbies.

Write a short article for the student website, explaining how you became interested in your favourite hobby and why others should take it up.

Student Ⓐ

I first got into snowboarding by watching it on TV. I'd never been skiing and for some reason I thought that was really boring but snowboarding looked exciting because it seemed more radical and to have a younger image. The snowboarders all looked really cool. As a result, I asked for a lesson for my birthday and found myself on an indoor slope.

I realized pretty quickly it wasn't as easy as it looked and you fall over a lot because your feet are strapped to the board. Consequently, I spent a lot of time falling on my face or on my bum, which really hurts.

However, the good thing is that you get the hang of the techniques much quicker than skiing. It's also easier to do jumps, so this makes it an exciting fast hobby. If you like skateboarding, you'd love snowboarding.

You don't need to buy special equipment for snowboarding, because you can hire everything at your local indoor slope or on holiday. One good reason to go to your local indoor slope first is to get the hang of the techniques. That way you don't waste a week of your holiday trying to learn what to do.

I love snowboarding because you get to whizz down mountains really fast! You can be travelling at 40 miles per hour just with the help of a piece of wood. When I first went snowboarding on holiday, I also loved the scenery. You experience the most amazing views and the snow is magical.

All in all, if you want to look cool and do something exciting, snowboarding is a really fun way to spend an hour or a week.

Begins to explain by giving reasons why and starts to use interesting vocabulary

Already starting to feel appropriate for a student audience

Clear paragraph with lots more explanation – the touch of humour is appropriate for the audience

More explanation, with a good comparison that the target audience might relate to; begins to address the second part of the question

More explanation about the hobby; useful detail; still using clear paragraphs

Brings back the focus to the first part of the question and uses some vocabulary for effect

Rounds this off effectively and uses direct address to make a final link with the audience

Skills workshop

As you discovered at the beginning of this chapter, you can also earn up to six marks for the accuracy of your writing.

Accurate spelling and punctuation, and use of Standard English and interesting sentences, are things you have been learning since you were very small. Bring them with you to the examination! Show the examiner what you have taken on board over the years to become a good communicator in English.

Here is the Mark Sceme that is used to mark your technical accuracy.

AO3, iii English AO4, iii English Language	Skills
Band 3 5–6 marks	<ul><li>uses sentence demarcation accurately and a range of punctuation with success</li><li>uses a variety of sentence forms to good effect</li><li>accurate spelling of more ambitious words</li><li>usually uses Standard English appropriately with complex grammatical structures</li></ul>
Band 2 3–4 marks	<ul><li>uses sentence demarcation which is mainly accurate with some control of punctuation</li><li>attempts a variety of sentence forms</li><li>some accurate spelling of more complex words</li><li>sometimes uses Standard English appropriately with some control of agreement</li></ul>
Band 1 1–2 marks	<ul><li>occasional use of sentence demarcation and punctuation</li><li>limited range of sentence forms</li><li>some accurate basic spelling</li><li>limited use of Standard English with limited control of agreement</li></ul>

Stepping stone to Band 2: sentence variety and punctuation

Think about the kinds of jobs sentences do in a piece of writing and then remember to punctuate them in the correct way.

Statement sentences or declaratives tell us something firmly. It may be factual or an opinion, but it comes across as logical and true. They end in full stops; for example, 'I have done my homework.'

Question sentences ask us something. They can sometimes be answered in your text; for example, you might use a question and answer format in a magazine interview. You might also use a question in a rhetorical way, perhaps as a subheading or something for your audience to think about. These end in question marks; for example, 'Should we do homework?'

Exclamations express an emotion – it could be positive (happiness or surprise) or more negative (shock or anger). This can be a useful way of creating a particular tone in your work, which might help you to score more highly for register. Exclamations end in exclamation marks; for example, 'It's the holidays. No more homework until September!'

Command sentences or imperatives tell us to do something. This may be a polite suggestion or an order. To suggest the action, the verb or action word comes first. They usually end in full stops, unless you want to suggest one of the moods mentioned above, in which case you can use an exclamation mark; for example, 'Do your homework, please./Do your homework!'

By aiming to use all four sentence functions in your text, with their correct punctuation marks, you will be able to show that you can:

- control some of your punctuation
- vary your sentence forms.

Try it yourself

Choose one of the sample Question 5 tasks below to practise your writing skills. Remember to:

- read the task carefully and work out precisely what is being asked of you
- check that you have identified the audience and the purpose
- think about the form you have been asked to write in and make a decision about your organization
- create a brief plan, for example, a spider diagram, flow chart or a list of ideas, before you begin to write
- try to write about a page
- complete your task in 25 minutes.

Activity 15

Complete one of the following Question 5-style tasks.

5 Write a feature article for a travel magazine, describing a good place for a family to visit in a half-term holiday.
(16 marks)

5 Write a letter to your school or college governors, explaining the changes you would like to see to make your school or college more responsible for the environment.
(16 marks)

5 Write a leaflet for students, informing them of the different leisure activities for young people in your local area.
(16 marks)

Self-assessment

Once you have completed your practice task, use this self-assessment feature to help you work out how well you have done and the areas you need to improve.

Self-assessment		
Organization		
Have I used paragraphs properly to mark the topic shifts in my writing?	Yes	No
Have I used the same layout features as a real text in this genre?	Yes	No
Content		
Is my piece of writing clear to read from beginning to end?	Yes	No
Have I used some details to make my piece of writing interesting?	Yes	No
Am I really sure about the purpose and have I stuck to it all the way through?	Yes	No
Have I used the right kinds of language features for this purpose?	Yes	No
Have I remembered who I am writing for and made it sound right for them?	Yes	No
Have I used really good vocabulary?	Yes	No
Accuracy		
Have I written in Standard English?	Yes	No
Have I used lots of different types of sentence to make the writing more interesting?	Yes	No
Have I remembered to punctuate my sentences?	Yes	No
Have I checked all my apostrophes?	Yes	No
Are all my basic spellings OK and my tricky words as good as I can get them?	Yes	No

What to expect in the exam

In the exam, you will be asked to complete two writing tasks. Question 6 is a longer writing task, worth 24 marks in total. It is worth more marks than any other Reading or Writing task on the paper.

You can earn up to 16 marks for the way you organize your piece of work and the way you communicate your ideas to your reader. You can also earn up to eight marks for how accurate your writing is. Look back at the list on page 80 to remind yourself how to do this.

A typical Question 6 task might look something like this:

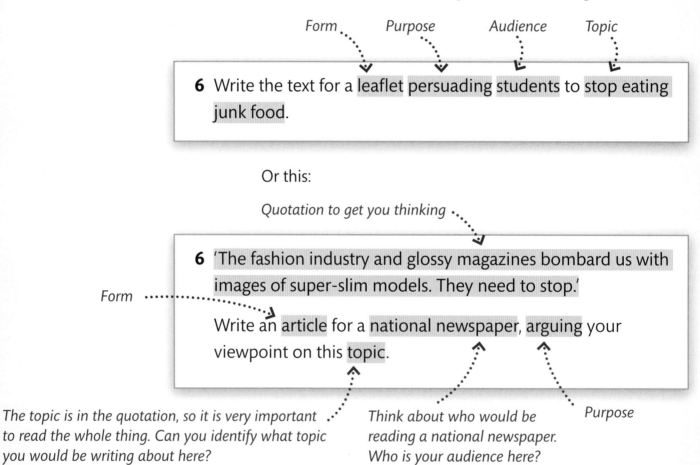

Form   *Purpose*   *Audience*   *Topic*

6 Write the text for a leaflet persuading students to stop eating junk food.

Or this:

Quotation to get you thinking

6 'The fashion industry and glossy magazines bombard us with images of super-slim models. They need to stop.'

Form

Write an article for a national newspaper, arguing your viewpoint on this topic.

The topic is in the quotation, so it is very important to read the whole thing. Can you identify what topic you would be writing about here?

Think about who would be reading a national newspaper. Who is your audience here?

Purpose

You will not get a choice of task in the exam, so read the question carefully, particularly if there is a quotation to read first. This is vital if you are to write about the correct topic.

You have 35 minutes to write Question 6, so spend five minutes planning. You are advised on the exam paper to 'try to write about a page'.

This task is worth a lot of marks. Do not be tempted to start writing without thinking and planning.

The content and organization of your work are marked using a Mark Scheme similar to the one used to mark Question 5, but the numbers of marks in the bands are different.

AO3, i, ii English AO4, i, ii English Language	Skills
Band 3 'clarity' 'success' 13–16 marks	**Content** • shows clarity of thought and communicates with success • engages the reader with more detail for purpose • clearly communicates the purpose • writes in a register which is clearly appropriate for audience • uses linguistic features appropriate to purpose • uses vocabulary effectively, including discursive markers **Organization** • uses paragraphs effectively in the whole text • uses a variety of structural features
Band 2 'some' 'attempts' 7–12 marks	**Content** • communicates ideas with some success • engages the reader with some detail for purpose • shows some awareness of the purpose • attempts to write in a register which is appropriate for audience • uses some linguistic features appropriate to purpose • attempts to vary vocabulary and use discursive markers **Organization** • uses paragraphs, which may be tabloid, at times correctly placed • some evidence of structural features
Band 1 'limited' 1–6 marks	**Content** • communicates with limited success • reference to one or two ideas linked to task • limited awareness of the purpose • limited awareness of the appropriate register for audience • simple use of linguistic feature(s) • uses simple vocabulary **Organization** • random or no paragraphs • limited use of structural features

Planning for a developed piece of writing

One of the key things an examiner is looking for in a Band 3 piece of writing is clarity. They are looking for:

- clear communication of your ideas
- a clear approach in the way you organize your work.

So, you need a method of planning that will help you organize both your ideas and the structure of your work.

Activity 1

1. With your class, look at the persuasive writing task below. What is the:

   a) form?

   b) audience?

   c) purpose?

   > You have just discovered that your local playing fields have been sold to a developer to build houses on.
   >
   > Write a letter to your local Member of Parliament, persuading them to campaign against this building project.

2. Student A has done some planning for this task (see the planning table, opposite). What has he done here to help get himself organized? How do you think this might help him to stay on-task?

3. Student A has gone on to plan five paragraphs for his letter (see the **topic sentences** table, opposite). Instead of planning the content of their paragraphs, what has Student A done?

Student Ⓐ

Planning table

	Form	Audience	Purpose
	Letter	MP	Persuade
Remember!	• Use paragraphs • Needs address • Needs Dear/ Yours faithfully	• Use formal register • Polite tone	• Rhetorical questions • Lists of three • Emotive language

Topic sentences table

Paragraph 1	I live in Greenbank and it has come to my attention that an estate of houses is going to be built on Greenbank Playing Fields.
Paragraph 2	The Greenbank Playing Fields are an important local facility.
Paragraph 3	I have many happy childhood memories of playing on these fields.
Paragraph 4	Building houses on these fields would have other damaging effects on our community.
Paragraph 5	I am asking you, as our MP, to support the campaign to stop the building.

Student A says:

I used to find it hard to get started on writing in exams. I get ideas for content but I waste time thinking of how to start. By planning like this, I have *topic sentences* that I can use as the first sentence in each of my paragraphs. It's easier to get started and I know how my writing will be structured. It's much easier when you know where the end will be before you begin! I don't waffle any more.

Activity 2

Choose one of the example tasks from page 106 and try this method for yourself.

1. Make a copy of the planning table above and fill in your form, audience and purpose. You should also fill in the things you know about:

   • how to structure your form

   • what your register might be.

2. Plan four or five paragraphs by writing your topic sentences.

Purpose: argue and persuade

The two **purposes** for Question 6 – **argue** and **persuade** – share many of the same features.

When we argue, we need to show the reader a point of view that they can think about and decide if they agree or disagree. In arguments, we have to use clear reasons and logic.

- We can present a one-sided argument, where we argue 'for' or 'against' an idea: for example, we might argue that school lunches should be healthier.

- Or we can present a balanced argument, where we show both sides of a topic: for example, we might argue whether or not we should spend more money on local sports facilities.

When we persuade, we need to give a powerful message and be convincing. We have to make it worthwhile for the reader to change their thoughts or behaviour, by showing them the benefits.

- For example, we might persuade someone to take part in a 10k run for charity or to give up smoking.

Key features of argument and persuasion

The key features of argument and persuasion are:

- Language features – the kinds of words and phrases you might choose

- Structural features – ways you might create memorable patterns in your sentences or 'sound effects' for the reader.

Together, these features are called rhetorical devices. Your task is to choose which of the rhetorical devices will help to make your piece of work more persuasive or will improve your argument. To help you do this, think carefully about your task and your audience.

Activity 3

The extract from the speech opposite was delivered by Earl Spencer at the funeral of his sister, Diana, Princess of Wales.

Make notes on the questions linked to some of the rhetorical devices he uses and then share your ideas.

Earl Spencer says he is representing three things here and puts them in a list. What are they and what do you notice about the order they come in?

He begins with the pronoun 'I' but changes in this sentence to using 'we' and 'our'. What reason might he have for doing that?

I stand before you today the representative of a family in grief, in a country in mourning before a world in shock.

We are all united not only in our desire to pay our respects to Diana but rather in our need to do so. For such was her extraordinary appeal that the tens of millions of people taking part in this service all over the world via television and radio who never actually met her, feel that they too lost someone close to them in the early hours of Sunday morning. It is a more remarkable tribute to Diana than I can ever hope to offer her today.

Why do you think Earl Spencer mentions this figure here?

Diana was the very essence of compassion, of duty, of style, of beauty. All over the world she was a symbol of selfless humanity.

Earl Spencer lists his sister's qualities. How does he make this list memorable for his listeners?

Earl Spencer uses three key rhetorical devices in his speech:

1. Pronouns:

- the first person pronoun 'I' – to show his individual viewpoint
- more inclusive pronouns 'we/our' – to include the listeners

2. Listing – to show the range of people affected and Diana's many qualities

3. Statistics – to emphasize the number of people who were paying their respects.

He has chosen these devices to suit the difficult task and to be sensitive to his audience.

Activity 4
. . . .

1. Add these three rhetorical devices (pronouns, listing and statistics) to the plan that you created in Activity 2. Include examples of pronouns, listing and statistics that you might use in your final response.

2. Write the opening paragraph of your chosen task, using your topic sentence and these three rhetorical devices to make it effective.

Exam tips

Often students have a whole checklist of devices to use in the argument or persuasive piece and write them in their plan.

However, they are not always appropriate for the task. Think about your audience and what you are trying to convince them of before adding devices to your work.

Developing your skills with rhetorical devices

Activity 5

Read the letter opposite, which was sent out as part of a charity campaign. It contains a number of rhetorical devices that have been annotated with questions for you to think about.

1. Discuss the questions with a partner and note down your responses.

2. Using your notes and the definitions in the table below, try to match every device with its name and definition.

An example has been done to help you get started.

Rhetorical device	Definition	Example from the text
Listing	A collection of three or more ideas separated by commas	...the end of their education, choices, dreams and opportunities
Inclusive pronouns	Pronouns that suggest something is shared and not individual	We, our
Rhetorical questions	A question used to make the listener think about a message or idea	
Anecdote	A personal story about someone or something	
Direct address	When a text speaks to the reader and involves them	
Statistics	Using numbers to make a text more factual	Every three seconds
Direct speech	Using the actual words a person involved in a topic might say	

Dear Mrs Jones

Will you give £18.80 to help keep a girl like Aneni in school and out of child marriage?

Can you remember what it was like to be 12 years old? Walking to school every morning with your best friend? Then playing together until your mum called you in?

Aneni is one girl who won't have childhood memories like this. She was taken out of school in Zimbabwe and forced to marry a man older than her father. Soon afterwards, she gave birth to his child – and all before her 13th birthday.

Every three seconds a girl like Aneni is forced into marriage, spelling the end of their education, choices, dreams and opportunities. Sadly, many endure abuse and violence.

Not only is this unjust. It's also a huge waste of potential.

That's why Plan is working with governments, teachers, parents and community leaders in developing an end to child marriage. We also support girls themselves to understand and claim their rights, and complete a quality education, so they, together with other girls and women, can be a force for change within their families and communities.

We are sure you'll agree, no girl should be forced into marriage. And we can't even begin to imagine what it must have been like for Aneni going through all she did at such a young age. Which is why we find it remarkable and inspirational that as a teenager she found the inner strength to put this ordeal behind her and join her local Plan child protection committee.

Aneni told us: 'I wouldn't want my children, or those from my community, to experience the pain and anguish I endured when I gave birth to my first child at the age of 12.'

Aneni is doing everything she can to help end child marriage. Will you help too?

This letter opens by asking you four things. How do you think the first question links to the other three? What connection is the writer asking you to make?

What is the impact of telling you the story of one girl here? Why do you think the letter uses her name?

Like the Earl Spencer text, there are statistics and listing here too. What different things do they show here?

By using this inclusive pronoun here, who is being referred to?

How does the letter try and get the reader on their side here?

This is a quotation from Aneni herself. It tells us something she has said about her own experience. How does this make the letter more persuasive for the reader?

Putting rhetorical devices into practice

Activity 6

1. Student A has written a complete response to the sample Question 6 task on page 108. Read the first paragraph of Student A's letter below and the notes alongside it.

2. Now read the next two paragraphs of the response (opposite) and identify the key rhetorical devices that Student A uses. Consider how they add to the persuasive effect of the letter.

3. Using the Mark Scheme on page 107 decide what mark you would award Student A for content and organization.

To help you, the examiner says:

> *This letter has a very clear structure. As well as showing the format of a letter, the paragraphs lead logically one from the other. There is a real variety of rhetorical devices to persuade the reader and a range of good points are made. The letter is polite, formal and has an appropriate register for a letter to an MP.*

Student A

48 Acaster Close
Northford
NO14 6XY

17 February 2013

Dear Mrs Smithson MP,

States the topic clearly and uses first person pronoun

Uses 'you' to address the MP directly and we/our to show that more than one person is unhappy about the building

Uses a list to add weight to the persuasion

Uses a statistic to give an indication of how the community might be affected

I live in Greenbank and it has come to my attention that an estate of houses is going to be built on Greenbank Playing Fields. I am writing to make you aware of how upset we, the local residents, are about this news and to invite you, our local MP, to join our campaign to stop this happening. The playing fields are used regularly by the whole community: dog walkers, children playing, the local 5-a-side squad, to name just a few. In our street alone, 20 out of 22 families said they regularly use this area in their leisure time. If building goes ahead this facility will be lost.

The Greenbank Playing Fields are an important local facility, I am sure you will agree, but they are also an important part of our local environment. The playing fields have many wildflowers and the hedges around them are home to lots of wild birds, including robins who come back to nest here every winter. A neighbour who is a member of the local conservation society recently told me that there are over 30 varieties of wildflower in this spot and as well as birds the fields are home to bees, butterflies and lizards.

I have many happy childhood memories of playing on these fields. If building goes ahead, local children will not just lose a place to play football but also a place to be in the countryside and see some of the natural world. Mrs Simmonds at the local primary school said, 'We often take the children to study insects and plants at Greenbank. We will be devastated if the land is built on. Many of our pupils do not have gardens of their own. This is an important part of their education.'

Activity 7

1. Using this letter as your Band 3 guide, revisit your opening paragraph for your practice task on junk food or super-slim models, adding any extra rhetorical devices where appropriate.

2. Write two more paragraphs of your answer thinking about:

- your structure and paragraphing

- your use of rhetorical devices

- how you can match your response to the Band 3 skills.

Key term

Tone The mood or feeling you create in your text. When we speak we use a tone of voice to convey our mood. In writing we can also show whether we are sympathetic, angry or being humorous through our tone.

Using the right tone

It's very important to get the **tone** of your argument or persuasive text right. Decide on your tone by thinking about:

- the topic of Question 6
- the audience for Question 6.

Some of the topics you may be asked to write about will be serious – a light-hearted tone or humour would not be appropriate.

Student A's letter to the MP on pages 114–115 uses a formal and polite tone. This is respectful to the person who is being addressed and it reflects the serious subject.

However, for other tasks your writing can be livelier. Humour can sometimes engage your audience and keep them on your side.

Crucially, remember that you aim to deliver strong messages both in arguments and persuasive pieces. You have to drive home your message, but don't be offensive or use humour inappropriately. You can show strong opinions and points of view, but avoid being rude or you will not win over your audience.

The two example texts on pages 117 and 118 deal with the topics of junk food and super-slim models. When you read them, think about how they create strong messages and powerful arguments for the reader.

Activity 8

Opposite is the opening of a script from the documentary film *Supersize Me*, in which Morgan Spurlock investigated the effects of junk food on people.

Read the extract from the script and discuss the questions in the annotations with a partner.

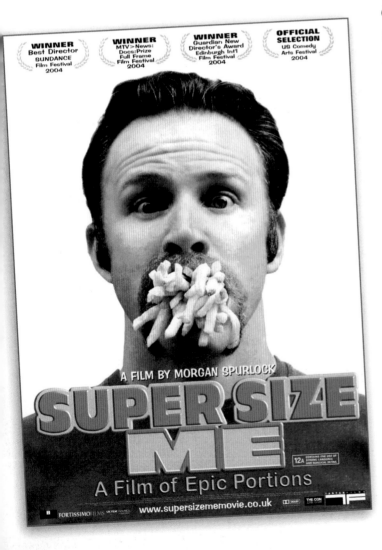

The writer creates a list here, but what is special about it? How is a memorable pattern created?

A very clear statement. What do you think the writer is trying to do here? How might an American audience feel when they hear this? Is the writer doing this on purpose?

A very powerful one word sentence. What tone might Morgan speak this in? Who is he congratulating and is he serious?

LIGHT FLUTE MUSIC PLAYS

Morgan: Everything's bigger in America. We've got the biggest cars, the biggest houses, the biggest companies, the biggest food, and, finally, the biggest people.

America has now become the fattest nation in the world.

Congratulations.

Nearly 100 million Americans are today either overweight or obese. That's more than 60% of all U.S. adults.

Since 1980 the total number of overweight and obese Americans has doubled, with twice as many overweight children and three times as many overweight adolescents.

The fattest state in America? Mississippi – where one in four people are obese.

I grew up in West Virginia, currently the third-fattest state in America. When I was growing up, my mother cooked dinner every single day. Almost all my memories of her are in the kitchen. And we never ate out, only on those few, rare special occasions. Today, families do it all the time, and they're paying for it – not only with their wallets, but with their waistlines.

Each day, one in four Americans visits a fast-food restaurant. And this hunger for fast food isn't just in America. It's happening on a global basis.

Why does the writer choose to use these statistics? Do you find anything shocking about them?

The writer asks a question here and answers it. What is the impact of that? How would you describe the tone of the question?

The writer has used the word 'fattest' three times. Why does he use this blunt vocabulary? Is he being offensive or rude?

The writer uses an anecdote about his own childhood. How does this comparison help his argument?

How does the alliteration in this sentence help to make the message more memorable?

What is interesting about this vocabulary choice?

Morgan Spurlock deals with a very controversial subject, but uses a number of rhetorical devices to back up his argument. He uses key facts and statistics and does not shy away from being blunt and shocking his reader. However, he is not rude or offensive. He is successful in delivering a very strong message.

Keeping it lively

This extract is from an article about celebrities gaining weight and presents a very different argument to the one in the *Supersize Me* script on page 117.

A size zero **dress does not equal success**

When Lady Gaga recently gained 25 pounds, the Internet went crazy posting the 'shocking' photos, along with derogatory comments and even speculating as to whether she may have packed on the pounds as a publicity stunt. Really? Who does that? In response to all the negative commentary, Gaga attributed the weight gain to simply eating too much pasta at her father's restaurant. But she also revealed that she has been suffering from eating disorders since she was 15.

Christina Aguilera was also in the news recently when she addressed her weight gain over the past year. She said that she had simply grown tired of constantly struggling to be super skinny in order to please record executives. She said that throughout her career, executives at her record label pressured her to remain thin and even went so far as to stage a weight intervention, but this time she told them, 'I'm fat. Deal with it.' She went on to say, 'They need a reminder sometimes that I don't belong to them. It's my body.'

This positive reinforcement is much needed. Young women – and some older ones as well – can't help but feel insecure as they leaf through the fashion magazines' portrayal of young women with airbrushed images that show an entirely unrealistic physical ideal. And even though we should know better by now, many of us are still comparing ourselves to that ideal.

So we thought our best response to the recent public scoldings these famous women are getting for putting on a few pounds is to remind us all that there are images of strength and success and beauty around us that are not airbrushed. And don't ask to be.

We all know that carrying too much weight can cause serious health problems. Obesity can lead to diseases that can threaten our lives. But that needn't force us to hold ourselves to one ideal. And, hey, who gets to decide what's beautiful? So let's remind ourselves and our daughters that achievement, talent and strength are beautiful in themselves. And that, by the way, physical beauty comes in a whole lot of sizes.

Like Morgan Spurlock, this writer develops ideas, uses a range of rhetorical devices and discusses a serious topic in a very convincing way.

The writer is informal in places and uses a lively tone, though the points are sharp and convincing.

Activity 9

1. Identify the rhetorical devices the writer uses to present her argument in the article opposite. You could collect them in a spider diagram or a list.

2. Which words or phrases in this article help to give it a lively tone?

3. The writer organizes her argument in paragraphs. Look at the topic sentence of each paragraph. What idea would you say is covered in each paragraph? Make a list of them like the example below.

> Paragraph 1: 'When Lady Gaga ... publicity stunt.' This paragraph uses a celebrity as an example of how the media make an issue out of people's weight.

4. Think about the key ideas in this argument:

   a) What message is the writer trying to give you about celebrities and their weight?

   b) What message is the writer trying to give you about ordinary people and their weight?

5. Compare your work on junk food or super-skinny models with the examples on pages 117 and 118. Write down three top tips you can take from the article and script to use in your final practice task.

Skills workshop

As you can see from the Mark Scheme below, you can earn up to eight marks in Question 6 by paying close attention to accuracy.

AO3, iii English AO4, iii English Language	Skills
Band 3 7–8 marks	• uses sentence demarcation accurately and a range of punctuation with success • uses a variety of sentence forms to good effect • accurate spelling of more ambitious words • usually uses Standard English appropriately with complex grammatical structures
Band 2 4–6 marks	• uses sentence demarcation which is mainly accurate with some control of punctuation • attempts a variety of sentence forms • some accurate spelling of more complex words • sometimes uses Standard English appropriately with some control of agreement
Band 1 1–3 marks	• occasional use of sentence demarcation and punctuation • limited range of sentence forms • some accurate basic spelling • limited use of Standard English with limited control of agreement

Stepping stone to Band 3: effective sentence forms and range of punctuation

There are different sentence types you can use to create special effects in your work. By using all four of the following sentence types, accurately punctuated, and thinking carefully about where and how they could be effective, you could move from Band 2 to Band 3 for your technical skills.

Simple sentences

All sentences begin with a main idea – a main idea with one clear action or verb in it. Sentences that are built like this are called simple sentences. They end with a full stop.

This is who is doing the action.   *This is the verb.*

The night is dark. The boy was running.

This is the noun connected to the action.   *This is the verb.*

Compound sentences

We can add another idea to our simple sentence by using a connective word like 'and', 'but' or 'so'. Joining two simple sentences together with connectives makes a compound sentence. This allows us to join up two ideas. Compound sentences end with a full stop.

The night was dark and the boy was running.

This is the connective which joins two simple sentences.

Complex sentences

We can also add detail and description to our main idea. We can add it before or after the main idea, or even before *and* after. This creates a complex sentence. Complex sentences end with a full stop, but use a comma or a pair of commas to separate the added detail from the main idea.

Here is the added detail.

Note the comma which separates the two.

Here is the main idea.

As darkness fell, the boy was running.

The boy was running, tripping over the branches in his path.

Added detail after the main idea.

As darkness fell, the boy was running, tripping over the branches in his path.

Note here we have a pair of commas either side of the main idea.

Minor sentences

A minor sentence is an interesting way of adding variety. Really, it isn't a sentence at all. It is a phrase that you want to draw attention to, to add drama to your writing, but you punctuate it with a full stop. A minor sentence does not need a verb.

The boy was running, panic-stricken and breathless.

It surrounded him. The dark night.

Can you identify the minor sentence here? What effect does it create?

Try it yourself

Choose one of the sample Question 6 tasks below to practise your writing skills. Remember to:

- read the task carefully and work out precisely what is being asked of you

- check that you have identified the form, audience and purpose and use this information to begin your planning table

- plan your topic sentences

- try to write about two pages

- complete your task in 35 minutes.

Activity 10

Complete one of the following Question 6-style tasks.

6 Write a speech for a college debate, arguing for or against raising the school-leaving age to 18.
(24 marks)

6 'A million TV channels, Xboxes, iPads and smartphones. We spend our lives looking at screens.'

Write an article for a magazine of your choice, persuading readers that technology is not always a good thing.
(24 marks)

Self-assessment

Once you have completed your practice task, use the self-assessment feature on page 105 to help you work out how well you have done and the areas you need to improve.

Section A: Reading

1. Read **Source 1**, the online article, 'Skyfall's Daniel Craig drops in on British troops in Afghanistan', and answer the questions below.

    a. List four things you learn about James Bond films from the article.

    (4 marks)

    b. What do you understand about Daniel Craig's visit to Afghanistan?

    Remember to:

    ● show your understanding by using your own words

    ● support your ideas with the text.   (4 marks)

2. Now read **Source 2**, an interview with Javier Bardem, an actor who plays the villain in the James Bond film, *Skyfall*.

    What do you understand about the actor Javier Bardem and his feelings about acting?

    Remember to:

    ● show your understanding of the text by explaining in your own words

    ● support your ideas with the text.   (8 marks)

3. Now read **Source 3**, 'Fifty Years of Bond', an article about the history of James Bond films.

    How does the writer use language features in the article?

    Remember to:

    ● give some examples of language features

    ● explain the effects.   (12 marks)

4. Now look again at **Source 1** and **Source 3**. Compare the way that they each use presentational features for effect.

    Remember to:

    ● write about the way the sources are presented

    ● explain the effect of the presentational features

    ● compare the way they look.   (12 marks)

Source 1

Culture > Film > Skyfall

Skyfall's Daniel Craig drops in on British troops in Afghanistan

Daniel Craig has paid a morale-boosting visit to British troops serving in Afghanistan as the latest 007 film, *Skyfall*, became the highest-earning James Bond film of all time.

Skyfall

....

Production year: 2012

Countries: Rest of the world, UK

Cert (UK): 12A

Runtime: 143 mins

Director: Sam Mendes

Craig's third film as the suave secret agent now has earnings of £421m worldwide. That is well ahead of the previous best tally for a Bond film, *Casino Royale*'s £375m in 2006.

Skyfall is the latest instalment in the series of films that began in 1962 with *Dr No*. It has emerged as one of the best-reviewed Bond films since the Sean Connery era. The film opened at No 1 at the US box office last weekend and took another £25.9m this weekend, putting it in second place behind the latest *Twilight* film.

Craig's surprise visit to Camp Bastion in Afghanistan was accompanied by a screening of the new film, *Skyfall*, for British troops. The actor, 44, joined 800 soldiers, sailors and airmen at the base, witnessing them in training.

He was able to take control of one of the state-of-the-art new armoured vehicles and apparently took the experience in his stride. 'We get quite a lot of visitors here, but having James Bond was special,' said Master Driver Rob Ingham after giving a demonstration. 'He seemed to be pretty comfortable in the driving seat.'

On a final stop, the actor was taught techniques used by explosives experts and search taskforce teams to look for roadside bombs. Squadron Sergeant Major Paul Ward said: 'His interest in the work of the soldiers is really appreciated.'

Javier Bardem on Hollywood, hair and being a Bond baddie

Javier Bardem has a face that was made to play a Bond villain: buggy eyes, crooked nose, full lips…

After the kinds of roles he has played – including the killer Anton Chigurh in *No Country For Old Men* – I wonder if it's possible that the actor finds himself sinister. 'Every time I wake up,' Bardem replies, and laughs loudly. 'I look at myself in the mirror to brush my teeth and it's very sinister. Ugh, look at that nose; look at those eyes. Ugh, my tone of voice.' Of course, as a movie star married to Penélope Cruz, he can afford to talk this way without fear of being taken at his word.

The 43-year-old and his wife, Penélope Cruz live in Madrid where, when he isn't acting, Bardem runs a bar with his sister. He grew up in a family of actors, but not in a glamorous way – most of his family, including his mother, were poor, frequently out of work and struggled to make ends meet.

When stars talk of what they 'sacrificed' to be successful, it makes Bardem cringe.

'Sacrifice to me has a different meaning. The background – your own history – is way more important than what you can achieve as a professional. My mother was an actress; and struggled to raise three children alone. She took second jobs. She cleaned stairs. Worked in a bingo hall. Many other things.'

'My grandfather and grandmother were actors. The parents of my grandparents were actors, in a time when actors were not allowed to be buried on sacred land. Terrible. My uncle is an actor, my brother is an actor and a writer, my sister used to be an actress. My cousins are actors. I've seen since I was born all that you can imagine in an actor's life. So I don't buy success. I don't buy failure. I only buy commitment.'

Being hired for the Bond movie, *Skyfall*, was a big deal, even though he'd been offered parts in previous Bond films.

There was a point during filming when Bardem appeared in a scene with both Judi Dench and Daniel Craig. 'And I looked at them both and forgot the lines. There was a silence and the director said, "Cut, what's wrong?" And I said, "I'm sorry, man, I just realized I'm in a James Bond movie and M and James Bond are looking at me."'

Source 3

Fifty Years of Bond

IT IS 50 YEARS since the then relatively unknown Scottish actor Sean Connery stepped onto our cinema screens, handsome and debonair, declaring, 'I'm Bond. James Bond.'

Little did that actor, or the directing team behind the massively successful box office blockbuster, know that Bond – in half a dozen different reincarnations – would be hitting our cinema screens for half a century.

In November, *Skyfall*, the 23rd official Bond movie was released and is now clocking up award after award, as well as breaking British box office records by grossing over £100 million. The world just can't seem to get enough of this very British hero, whose charm and charisma help him out of more sticky situations than the array of spy gadgets that have become just one of his trademarks.

Six actors have taken on the role of Bond so far and Daniel Craig is currently following in the famous footsteps of Pierce Brosnan, Timothy Dalton and George Lazenby. Up until now, it is Roger Moore's 1970s Bond and Sean Connery's Bond of the swinging 60s that have most captured our imaginations, but Craig's icy blue stare and his cool charm

seem set to leave the Bond cocktail shaken, not stirred, for some years to come.

Bond is, without a doubt, a cultural icon, though he seems to symbolize a British style that only the lucky few possess. A snappy dresser in statement sunglasses, an expert at the roulette wheel, as well as the wheel of an Aston Martin or Lotus Elise, Bond is impeccable in his manners and his tastes.

Bond travels the world – the films take us from the most glamorous European destinations, snow-capped Switzerland and millionaire's playground Monaco, to far flung exotic locations in Jamaica and the Bahamas.

He meets the most beautiful women, though many are as much his enemy as his ally.

He encounters the most terrifying of villains, Goldfinger, Scaramanger and Blofeld, the notorious and deadly leader of SPECTRE.

And yet, he survives; he walks away, cool, calm and collected, reassuring us that we are safe on our little island, as long as suave secret agents in pristine tuxedos continue to sip vodka martinis and announce to the enemy in cut-glass Queen's English, 'I'm Bond. James Bond.'

Section B: Writing

5. The character James Bond is famous for escaping from difficult situations. Choose a time when you faced a difficult situation and write an entry for your journal, diary or blog, explaining how you overcame it.

Remember to:

● write a diary/journal or blog entry

● use language to explain.

Try to write approximately one page.   (16 marks)

6. 'Young people today witness too much violence in films and video games.' Write an article for a national newspaper, arguing for or against this statement.

Remember to:

● write an article

● use language to argue.

Try to write approximately two pages.   (24 marks)

OXFORD
UNIVERSITY PRESS

Great Clarendon Street, Oxford OX2 6DP

Oxford University Press is a department of the University of Oxford. It furthers the University's objective of excellence in research, scholarship, and education by publishing worldwide in

Oxford New York

Auckland Cape Town Dar es Salaam Hong Kong Karachi
Kuala Lumpur Madrid Melbourne Mexico City Nairobi
New Delhi Shanghai Taipei Toronto

With offices in

Argentina Austria Brazil Chile Czech Republic France Greece
Guatemala Hungary Italy Japan South Korea Poland Portugal
Singapore Switzerland Thailand Turkey Ukraine Vietnam

Oxford is a registered trade mark of Oxford University Press in the UK and in certain other countries

© Oxford University Press 2013

Database right Oxford University Press (maker)

First published 2013

British Library Cataloguing in Publication Data

Data available

ISBN 978-019-839038-1

10 9 8 7 6 5 4 3 2 1

Printed in Great Britain by Bell and Bain Ltd., Glasgow

Acknowledgements

The publisher and author are grateful to the following for permission to reproduce photographs:

Cover, p2, p4 & p78: Ijansempoi/Shutterstock

Photos: **p7**: Prof. Indraneil Das; **p9l**: Eric Isselee/Shutterstock; **p9r**: Kappleyard/Shutterstock; **p11 & p15**: Renate Micallef/Shutterstock; **p13**: robas/iStock; **p14**: Christine Langer-Pueschel/Shutterstock; **p16**: luxorphoto/Shutterstock; **p19**: Markus Gann/Shutterstock; **p20**: Lebrecht Music and Arts Photo Library/Alamy; **p23**: ronfromyork/Shutterstock; **p24-25**: chaoss/Shutterstock; **p26**: PCN Photography/Alamy; **p30**: Jennifer Stone/Shutterstock; **p32**: Shukaylova Zinaida/Shutterstock; **p34**: FocusEurope/Alamy; **p38**: Ivonne Wierink/Shutterstock; **p39**: Janine Wiedel Photolibrary/Alamy; **p41**: Jostein Hauge/Shutterstock; **p43l**: KathyGold/Shutterstock; **p43r**: iurii/Shutterstock; **p45**: Edyta Pawlowska/Shutterstock; **p46tr**: The National Trust; **p46l**: Cosmin Manci/Shutterstock; **p46mr**: Ian Rentoul/Shutterstock; **p46br**: auremar/Shutterstock; **p47tl**: USBFCO/Shutterstock; **p47tr**: Arvind Balaraman/Shutterstock; **p47b**: agebroom/Shutterstock; **p48**: Eric Isselee/Shutterstock; **p50**: keith morris/Alamy; **p51**: stocker1970/Shutterstock; **p53**: Arieliona/Shutterstock; **p57**: Catalyst Discovery Centre; **p59**: Cats Protection League; **p61 & p62**: Barcroft Media; **p64**: Barcroft Media; **p67 l-r**: The National Trust; British Heart Foundation (BHF logo); Amnesty International; **p69**: www.helpforheroes.org.uk; **p70**: Matt Cardy/Getty Images; **p73**: www.helpforheroes.org.uk; **p76**: Spaceport Discovery Centre; **p77**: Wildfowl & Wetlands Trust; **p85**: Oleksiy Mark/Shutterstock; **p86**: Monkey Business Images/Shutterstock; **p88**: Volodymyr Goinyk/Shutterstock; **p89t**: Sergey Uryadnikov/Shutterstock; **p89b**: viki2win/Shutterstock; **p90**: Goodluz/Shutterstock; **p91**: Bartek Zyczynski/Shutterstock; **p92**: Deborah Benbrook/Shutterstock; **p94**: Getty Images; **p97**: Snvv/Shutterstock; **p99**: David Crosbie/Shutterstock; **p102**: Monkey Business Images/Shutterstock; **p104**: dotshock/Shutterstock; **p108-109**: Toncsi/Shutterstock; **p111**: Rex Features; **p115**: Mat Hayward/Shutterstock; **p116**: Ronald Grant Archive; **p117**: johnfoto18/Shutterstock; **p118**: s_bukley/Shutterstock.com; **p122**: Piti Tan/Shutterstock; **p124**: Corporal Neil Bryden RAF/Rex Features; **p125**: c.Col Pics/Everett/Rex Features; **p126t**: Bettmann/CORBIS; **p126b**: John Springer Collection/CORBIS

The publisher and author are grateful to the following for permission to reprint extracts from copyright material:

Abel & Cole Ltd for recipe for 'Saucy Spring Greens' from www.abelandcole.co.uk

Anness Publishing Ltd for 'Flower Friends Project' from *Gardening Projects for Kids* by Jenny Hendy (Southwater, 2011).

ESI Media, London Evening Standard for Hettie Harvey: 'Dane Dream: Falling for Handsome Copenhagen', *London Evening Standard*, 21.9.2012, copyright © London Evening Standard 2012.

Guardian News and Media for 'Javier Bardem: Sinister? Me?' by Emma Brockes, *The Guardian*, 12.10.12, copyright © Guardian News & Media Ltd 2012; 'Skyfall's Daniel Craig drops in on British Troops in Afghanistan' by Ben Child, *The Guardian*, 19.11.12, copyright © Guardian News & Media Ltd 2012; 'German Police release photo of mystery "forest boy"' by Kate Connolly, *The Guardian*, 13.6.12, copyright © Guardian News & Media Ltd 2012; and 'Help for Heroes new rehab centre: 'This is a launchpad for life'' by Steven Morris, *The Guardian*, 18.10.12, copyright © Guardian News & Media Ltd 2012.

David Higham Associates for Roald Dahl: *Boy: Tales of Childhood* (Penguin, 2008), and *Going Solo* (Penguin, 2008).

National Trust for 'Bear Grylls, explorer, author and Chief Scout', *National Trust Magazine*, No 123, Summer 2012, and 'Explore Brownsea Island' leaflet, text copyright © National Trust 2012.

The Octagon Theatre, Bolton for extract from pantomime leaflet for *Peter Pan* at The Octagon, Nov 2012-Jan 2013.

Pan Macmillan Ltd for *Red Dust Road* by Jackie Kay (Picador, 2010), copyright © Jackie Kay 2010.

Plan UK for Appeal Letter.

Solo Syndication for 'One Whale of a Tail' by Nadia Gilani, and photo caption from *Metro*, 5.10.2012.

Telegraph Media Group for 'Surge in number of men o' war being washed up on beaches' by David Millward, *Daily Telegraph*, 8.9.2012, copyright © Telegraph Media Group Ltd 2012.

The Wildlife Trusts for *152 Wild Things to Do* (Elliott & Thompson/ The Wildlife Trusts, 2010).

Although we have made every effort to trace and contact all copyright holders before publication this has not been possible in all cases. If notified, the publisher will rectify any errors or omissions at the earliest opportunity.

Author acknowledgements

Thank you to Brian for technical assistance and tea. Thank you to Alex and Lydia for going to bed on time during the production of this book.